Straight Up,
Life With A Twist

QUOTES

i

FAN MAIL FROM OUR FRIENDS

"Neither abstinence nor excess ever made a person happy. What a good healthy look at drinking your book affords us,"

— *Joshua Berkhoven, New York.*

I've tried all of your hangover cures and none of them work,"

— *Robert Johnson, Glasgow.*

"It was a delight to find out how much influence the Culpepper family had on the development of social drinking. But before the Culpeppers could hold a family reunion, they would have to own a brewery, a distillery and a football stadium,"

— *Eve Bottomley, Toronto. (Ed.'s note: they do!)*

"The World's 10 Best Pickup Lines has helped me meet some interesting people in some interesting situations,"

— *John Bron, Los Angeles*

"Nothing ever tastes better than a cold beer on a beautiful afternoon with nothing to look forward to but more of the same. Thank you for not making me feel guilty about it,"

— *Jim "Dingo" Hammond, Melbourne, Australia*

"What a toffee-nosed pain in the butt you are Mr. Culpepper, la-dee-dahing on about how to open a bottle of champagne. In the cavalry, we took our sabers and lopped the top off. The ladies loved it,"

— *Major Christian Jeffrey, Chicago*

The Bachelor's Guide™ to *LIBATIONS!*

By Clarence "Cocktail" Culpepper

THE BACHELOR'S GUIDE™ TO LIBATIONS
By Clarence "Cocktail" Culpepper

First Printing – October 1995

Copyright© 1995

Normac Publishing Ltd.
4104 - 149 Street
Edmonton, Alberta
Canada T6H 5L9

Canadian Cataloguing in Publication Data

Culpepper, Clarence "Cocktail" (Nick Lees),

  The bachelor's guide to libations

  Includes index.
  ISBN 1-895292-59-X
1. Bartending. 2. Alcoholic beverages.
3. Entertaining. I. Jones, Yardley, 1930-
II. Title.

TX951.C84 1995   641.8'74   C95-920204-8

Illustrations by
Yardley Jones

Designed, Printed and Produced in
Canada by:
Centax Books,
a Division of PrintWest Communications Ltd.
Publishing Director: Margo Embury
1150 Eighth Avenue, Regina, Saskatchewan,
Canada S4R 1C9
(306) 525-2304
FAX (306) 757-2439

TABLE OF CONTENTS

FOREWORD

We would like to thank the ancient Babylonians and early Egyptians for making this book possible.

Had they not found out respectively how to brew beer from malted barley and make wine, civilization might have been held back thousands of years and a sophisticated book such as this would not have been possible.

We would also like to thank those who worked on improving the taste of fermented grape juice after finding their concoctions didn't make them as sick as their lousy water.

And a big thanks must go to the Roman Catholic monks who tended their vines so meticulously that communicants enjoyed a top-notch tipple every Sunday.

More recently, we would like to thank:

- Smuggler's Inn Liquor Connoisseur, Tim Warman,
- Susanne Wood (Aide de Livre)
- The female editorial staff at the Edmonton Journal who unstintingly revealed the best and worst pickup lines they had ever heard.
- Spyder Yardley – Jones (still a bachelor)
- Al Hauptman, Westmount Liquor Service, Purveyor of Fine Spirits

To all those "bachelors" at heart out there,
old and young,
the flame always flickers.

INTRODUCTION
BY CLARENCE
"COCKTAIL" CULPEPPER

"Thunder is good, thunder is impressive, but it's lightning that does the work." Mark Twain wasn't thinking of your entertaining a lovely lady at your pad when he penned those words. But his message works. You may be able to prepare one heck of a meal for your date, but there is one important thing that is going to help you maximize the evening's potential. ("Wink, wink, nudge, nudge, say no more, know what I mean?" as they said in Monty Python's Flying Circus.) You need to know about libations.

You've probably found some fabulous recipes in your *Bachelor's Guide™ to Ward Off Starvation* cookbook and are now a whizz at preparing them. But what you need are a few sound tips about the drinks you should serve; some cocktail and shooter recipes; a few party ideas; a party check list; a selection of toasts and a few suggestions about bar gear.

In case your date really doesn't like to get merry on the product of juice-filled grapes and sun-ripened grains, we have a special chapter on nonalcoholic drinks.

By the time you have finished this book, women will think you know more about drinks than the sommelier at London's swank Savoy Hotel. Hopefully you will get your just desserts at the end of the evening. To all you bachelors out there . . . lots of luck and good hunting, prosit, skoal, a votre santé, ¡salude!, salute, bottoms up and cheers, to mention but a few.

As sincerely as possible,

Clarence "Cocktail" Culpepper

Clarence "Cocktail" Culpepper

BEER

BEER

Beer is probably the world's oldest alcoholic drink. So if it was good enough for the Babylonians and the Egyptians more than 6,000 years ago, it's probably a good bet when it comes to impressing your dinner date. It's no accident that it is the drink of choice at baseball and football games. They've had time to get the wrinkles out and make it darn near perfect.

It's hard to know what a women will ask for with so many good beers on the market nowadays, so it's probably best to have several types on hand.

I once dated a lovely lass from the north of England who wouldn't come over and watch wrestling on television unless I had a case or two of Newcastle Brown in the house.

And then there was Cynthia, a bank teller who fancied herself as a model. She always asked for a light beer because it was lower in calories. But she would eat three bags of potato chips, half a pound of cheese and a couple of bowls of peanuts while I was making her favorite skinless turkey-breast-and-vegetable casserole cooked in chicken consomme. While we have all done it from time to time under pressure, it's not a good idea to pour a beer for your lady friend into the glass you have just drained. It doesn't matter if she arrived early and caught you on the wrong foot. She won't mind if you take an extra second or two to get a spotless glass. Spots and streaks are always very noticeable. It's worth remembering that the head of beer collapses in a greasy glass.

When it comes to drinking beer, don't be afraid to have a real good gulp. Farmers, firemen and fighter pilots don't have a pinkie in the air and sip gently while quenching their thirst at the end of the day. They belt it back. As proof of this, the scholarly Professor Higgins Culpepper was fond of quoting from Charles Dickens' *Old Curiosity Shop*.

"Did you ever taste beer?"
"I has a sip of it once," said the small servant.
"Here's a state of things!" cried Mr Swiveller.
"She never tasted it – it can't be tasted in a sip!"

Here's some conversational stuff you can dazzle her with as you whip up something from your Bachelor's Guide™ cookbook.

Beer, you can tell her, is usually made from malted barley flavored with hops. It became the beverage of choice in northern climes where grapes couldn't be grown.

Beer and wine are both fermented and undistilled, but while wine is made from materials high in sugar content, beer is brewed from starchy materials. The starches must be converted to sugar before fermentation can occur.

Other grains, such as rice, corn or wheat are also sometimes used to make beer. In Africa, hundreds of beer-type drinks are made from such materials as millet, sorghum and other crops.

The Japanese and Mexicans both export some pretty fair suds these days. But there's no reason why you shouldn't make your own. Stores that sell beer-and-wine-making equipment are opening everywhere. Check the Yellow Pages. It's easy to make beer and you'll find the stuff in these stores very helpful. They have a vested interest in you doing well. They want you to come back for more supplies. Making your own beer can cut the cost of a case of suds quite significantly. If you make a batch that doesn't taste quite right, mix it with a few bottles from the store and introduce it late in the evening

to a party that's already shaking.

Here's a quick reference guide to some types of beer:

ALE: This is a stronger, yummy beer that is popular in England and Ireland. It is brewed at a higher temperature, causing the yeast to float to the top of the vat, rather than settle, as in the case of lagers. Carbon dioxide is released and rises to the top to form a head. Robin Hood and his band always grabbed a barrel or two of ale when they rescued Maid Marion from the Sheriff of Nottingham's castle.

WE RESCUED THE ALE — BUT DARN! WE'VE FORGOTTEN MAID MARIAN AGAIN!

CAN'T WIN 'EM ALL!

LAGER: This light, foaming, aged brew, is the most popular beer in North America. It takes its name from the German *Lagern*, which means "to store." Some 1,400 years ago or so, monks found beer kept better during warm summer months if it was stored in dank mountain caves. They also found it mellowed with age. Lagers are high in carbonation and are usually between 3 and 5 percent in alcohol content by volume. Many imported European beers are also lagers. They tend to be a tad tastier than the stuff churned out by big North American breweries.

STOUT: This is another dark beer, but it is usually rich, with pronounced flavors of malt and hops. It can also be a tad sweet. Guinness, from Ireland, is a champion in this class. (Ale, stout and porter usually range in alcohol content from 4 to 6.5 percent or more by volume.)

PORTER: This is a dark English beer noted for its rich and heavy foam. Porter is between ale and stout in flavor. Many of the microbreweries springing up in North America are now making a very palatable drop of porter.

BOCK BEER: Darker, sweeter and stronger than the lagers, bock beer is brewed in the late winter and stored until spring. Bock beer was first brewed by the Germans, but its popularity has spawned many imitations.

LIGHT BEER: Brews of this type have fewer calories and less alcohol. But this is at the expense of flavor.

SHANDY: Short for shandygaff, a mixture of beer and another beverage, such as ginger beer, lemonade, ginger ale, Sprite or 7-Up. (Very popular after rugby games when players seek to restore their electrolyte balance.)

ICE-FILTERED BEER: This ice-filtered beer is the new boy on the the beer block. Labatt's, in Canada, started the ice filtration process and its popularity has quickly spread around the world.

WINE

WINE

Ernest Hemingway, perhaps one of the greatest womanizers of them all, loved a glass of wine. When he lived in Paris, he'd often finish his writing by midday and head for a cafe en route to the race track.

What would he drink? Pouilly-Fuissé, an outstanding white Burgundy made from the chardonnay grape.

Wine to him was a wonderfully sensuous drink, with its history, geography, climate and soil all playing their role in the nectar he lovingly sniffed and sipped.

Count Culpepper, who lived a stone's throw from St. Julien in fine Bordeaux country, was also a great fan of wine and said he found grape juice aphrodisiacal.

"At the very mention of Château Lafite, Château Margaux or Château Haut-Brion, I feel my manhood aroused," he said. "I'm afraid to walk in my cellar nowadays in case I suffer a heart attack."

But wine was ever thus. It even had a history by the time the Old Testament was written. In Genesis 9:20 it was ascribed to Noah.

The Greeks kept their wine in casks, goatskins and earthenware containers, and stoppered them with oil or a greasy rag. But it was the Romans who planted vines wherever they went and it was the monks who lovingly tended them because wine was necessary for communion.

12

Countless books on wine fly off the presses every year, so in the limited space here, I'm giving you a primer on wine that may be to your advantage should your lady friend like to join you in working up to a frenzy just by talking about wine. (It's surprisingly how many do.)

Wine is usually made from the fermented juices of grapes, the major constituents being water, sugar and alcohol. But more than 400 known compounds contribute to the flavor, aroma and color of wine. And that's why wine from the same grape but from various countries can taste so very differently.

While you can pay hundreds of dollars for a bottle of Château Latour and think it worth while if it brings about your desired state of bliss, don't overlook wines that nowadays come in foil containers. They are colorful, fit easily into the cooler, don't break when bounced and are very competitively priced. Don't put them on the table if you are serving a candlelight dinner, but pour a glass in the kitchen, sniff the aroma lovingly and hand it to your impressed date.

There are good red wines and good white wines. People spend fortunes and their lifetimes trying to find out which one they like the most. I have yet to find a bad one.

Today's lesson is taken from 1 Timothy, Verse 23: "Drink no longer water, but use a little wine for thy stomach's sake."

A DAY WITHOUT WINE IS LIKE A DAY WITHOUT SUNSHINE!

If you need a second opinion, here's Louis "Pasteurization" Pasteur: "Wine is the most healthful and most hygienic of beverages." To back that up, recent research has shown that the French, who love great rich, buttery sauces and cheeky cheeses, don't suffer the same number of heart casualties as other developed countries that enjoy a similar lifestyle.

The reason? The French love their wines and scientists believe there's something in wine that helps guard against heart problems.

If you need one more reason to uncork a bottle, remember that old French cliché, a day without wine is like a day without sunshine.

SHERRY: Sherry is fortified by the addition of brandy. It is fermented and aged in gigantic casks of white oak.

VERMOUTH: The dry, pale Vermouth and the sweet dark Vermouth are taken straight or are used in martinis and Manhattans. Many people like them on the rocks with a twist. Vermouths are also fortified wines and are flavored with herbs and aromatics.

DUBONNET: Flavored with herbs and quinine, this is a sweet apéritif, a sort of premeal appetizer.

I'M NOT QUESTIONING ITS SCATHINGLY IMPUDENT BOUQUET ITS PROVOCATIVE AFTERTASTE, OR EVEN ITS TANTALIZING FRUITINESS — I JUST WANT SOMETHING TO GO WITH MACARONI LEFTOVERS!

LIKE, HAVE A BEER, EH?

TASTING

Here are six ways you can judge a wine.

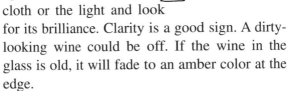

1. LOOK: Once you have poured a little wine into a glass, hold it against a white table-cloth or the light and look for its brilliance. Clarity is a good sign. A dirty-looking wine could be off. If the wine in the glass is old, it will fade to an amber color at the edge.

2. SWIRL: Swirl the wine in the glass – easy does it – to release the aroma by bringing oxygen into contact with your chosen grape juice.

3. AROMA: A connoisseur can tell by the smell of a wine whether it is good or not. The taste is the final confirmation. Hold the glass up to your nose and inhale deeply. With practice, you will be able to pick up different characteristics, such as spices, fruit, tobacco, herbs and so on. Half the fun of wine is in recognizing different aromas and comparing the bottle with others you have enjoyed. A stinky or chemical-smelling wine may be off. Return it.

4. SIP: Drag as much air as you can into your mouth as you sip a wine and let the wine roll over your tongue, from side to side.

5. SAVOR: Enjoy the taste and remember it. Does a white wine taste of lemons or a red one of black currants? It doesn't take a lot of practice before you can tell immediately whether a wine has good body and is well balanced or should be used for cooking.

6. SWALLOW: Swallow and enjoy. A good, well-made intense wine will linger. Upstarts will vanish quickly from your taste buds.

BUYING

There is no such thing as a good wine or a bad wine. "You pays your money and you takes your pick," as secondhand-car dealer Shylock Culpepper used to say. If you like a $5 bottle of blended Hungarian wine, you are very lucky, and should be the envy of people who can't make do with anything less than a $30 château-bottled job.

Shop around and compare prices. Check items on sale. A store will often sell off "bin ends" at a reduced price. That's a few remaining bottles of a particular wine that they want to move to make room for a new order.

A good tip is to find a wine store where you feel comfortable. Ask the staff for advice, mentioning the sum you'd like to spend.

Wine should be stored in a cool area where it isn't subject to great fluctuations in temperature. It should also be placed on its side to keep the cork moist and to help prevent air getting in. If you don't store wine properly, you might find yourself sipping vinegar.

WHITES

Most people start off drinking white wine, often the sweeter types. But as tastes develop, the senses often seem to appreciate a dryer, finer, more complex wine. But you are the sole judge of what is good or bad.

At one time, people said white wine went with white meat and that red wine was to be consumed with red meat. That's not exactly true. Drink what you like and enjoy it.

Here are some of the world's best-known white grape types. Champagne deserves and gets its own chapter, please see page 22. Remember, champagne is about the only drink that tastes good at any time of the day and can be consumed with any dish. It harmonizes with hors d'oeuvres, steak and chocolate.

CHARDONNAY (Char-doe-nay): This grape has enjoyed a tremendous rise in popularity over the last couple of decades and prompted white wine growers the world over to plant chardonnay vines. Chardonnays can have tremendous finesse and elegance. Some of the world's greatest white Burgundy wines, such as Montrachet, Meursault, Chablis and Pouilly-Fuissé, are chardonnays. The transplanted grape has done well all over the world, particularly in California and Australia. If Chardonnay wine has been aged in oak, it has a wonderfully smoky, woody flavor. Terrific with the heavier sea offerings, such as salmon and lobster, it also goes well with chicken and veal.

RIESLING (Reese'-ling): If you drink wine, you've almost certainly had a Riesling. The grape is used for the great wines of the Rhine and Mosel in Germany and some of the best wines from Alsace in France. Typically, Rieslings are honey/flowery-flavored wine with a hint of herbaceous

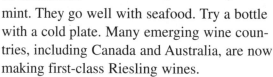

mint. They go well with seafood. Try a bottle with a cold plate. Many emerging wine countries, including Canada and Australia, are now making first-class Riesling wines.

SAUVIGNON BLANC (So'-veen-yawn Blawn'): An excellent white grape used along with Semillion in Bordeaux to produce the fine dry white Graves and Entre-Deux-Mers. The grape is also used to make such sweet wines as Sauternes and Barsac, and the dry white wines of Pouilly-Fumé and Sancerre. The wine's abundant acid tends to give it a delicious tart finish, which adds to robust flavors of fruit and spice. If you're a real man and love quiche, this might be the wine to go with it.

REDS

Tradition has it that red wines should be served at "room temperature." But when that decree went out, homes tended to be much colder. Many red wines are shown to best advantage if they are chilled slightly before drinking.

I THINK YOU'LL FIND THE BRONTOSAURUS DRIPPLE DIPPLE HAS ALMOST A BRONZE AGE AFTER TASTE!

Portugal and South Africa are the two new kids on the block offering well-made wines at good prices.

BEAUJOLAIS (Boo'-zho-lay): Beaujolais is your good wine all-rounder. It goes with darn near anything and is usually fairly well priced. It offers an explosion of fresh fruity qualities. But the wine doesn't last and should be drunk during its first year. It's a good introduction to red wine. Definitely serve slightly chilled.

CABERNET SAUVIGNON (Cab'-air-nay So'-vin-yawn): This grape is Churchillian in strength and character and usually requires some aging in cask or bottle. The great Bordeaux of France usually feature this grape, which has adapted well to such places as California, Australia, Chile, Italy, South Africa and Bulgaria. Good cabernets are pretty intense and are the perfect wines to accompany everything from a hamburger to a T-bone.

PINOT NOIR (Pee'-no Nwahr): This is the grape used to make the great Burgundies. Three-fourths of all champagne is also made from Pinot Noir. More brilliant in color than Bordeaux, the wines also tend to age faster. The vine is quite demanding as to soil and growing season. They often have a slightly sweet bouquet, a woody nose and a wonderful **19**

fruity taste. Perfect with duck and other types of game.

SYRAH (Sir-rah'): A big grape native to the Rhone Valley in France, it makes robust wines that are often blended with others to round them out. Châteauneuf-Du-Pape, a favorite red of many, is blended with up to 13 different varieties. Syrah-based wines usually have a slightly higher alcohol content, which makes them warm and a great accompaniment to stews and casseroles. Most Côtes du Rhone Villages (France) are worth a try. The grape is known as Shiraz in Australia.

CHIANTI (Key-ahn'-tee): This famous red wine from Tuscany, Italy, was one of the world's first dry reds. It kisses, bites, thrusts and stings the palate in its youth. (Sound familiar?) The better ones are velvety smooth when they are aged. The wine was traditionally associated with a hand-blown squat, straw-covered flask. Labor costs have largely taken care of that.

RIOJA (Ree-o'-ha): Riojas are usually of outstanding value. The wines come from a dry, mountainous region in northern Spain that has similar conditions to those in Bordeaux. When the disease phylloxera ravaged the French vineyards in the late 19th century, many French winemakers took their centuries-old techniques to the Rioja. Soft, oaky, fruity and with some vanilla flavoring, a good Rioja Reserve is the wine for lamb, beef, pork, game meats, stews and casseroles.

PORT

This is the perfect drink to serve at the end of a meal, accompanied by some English Stilton and grapes. But once opened, you must tell your lady friend, a bottle of port must be drunk or it will spoil. It's time to

move to the sofa, turn the lights down and play romantic music. An Italian tenor singing an aria, a French chanteuse singing about a lost lover, or if you have one piece of symphony music, now is the time to play it.

Port is a rich, fruity, heavy-bodied sweet dessert class wine. It is usually deep red, but can be tawny or white in color. It was developed at the beginning of the 18th century when the British, who were trading woolens to the Portuguese for wine, protested, saying the wine was too harsh.

But English wine merchants at Oporto found that if they added grape brandy, before all the grape sugar had fermented out, they could satisfy the buddies at home with a wine that was sweeter. Port caught on big time and the Brits sold the stuff around the world.

For more than a century, port was the best-known wine in Britain and the only wine allowed in some conservative households.

"Ruby" and "tawny" ports are blends that have been matured in wood using as many as 30 types of port. Tawny is aged longer, losing some of its red color as sediment is regularly strained out.

CHAMPAGNE

VENEZ VITES FRÉRES JE BOIS DES ÉTOILES!
(COME QUICKLY MY BROTHERS, I AM DRINKING THE STARS!)

DOM PÉRIGNON (17th CENTURY BENEDICTINE MONK UPON TASTING HIS DISCOVERY- THE CHAMPAGNE PROCESS)

CHAMPAGNE

A gentlemen entertaining a lady at home, on a picnic, at sea, in a mountain cabin or in a ski condo, could do no better than surprise her with "a bottle of bubbly."

Ahh, the bubbles and froth!

The excitement as the chilled, pale-gold liquid is poured into a flute. It's champagne, the best known of all the world's wines. It's the perfect drink to serve at any time to make a moment special. And it's the only wine that tastes good with every type of food.

Champagne comes from a hillside area in northeastern France, roughly a triangular area connecting Reims, Epernay and Châlons-sur-Marne. Only wine from this area may be called "Champagne." Other French sparkling (bubbly) wines are called "vins mousseux." (Pronounced: "van moose-oh!")

Champagne has been perfected through the centuries and its success has spawned many an imitation. But other makers of wine using the same process can, by law, only say on their label "methode champenoise," not champagne.

Pinot noir and chardonnay are the main types of grapes used in making champagne. A few drops of a sweet liqueur, which determines sweetness, is added before the bottle is strongly corked. The cork is wired in.

It's important to try and put a little majesty into the opening a bottle of champagne, or any sparkling wine. So plan ahead.

Being a white wine, champagne should be served chilled. Pop the bottle of champagne into the refrigerator (not the freezer) at least an hour before you plan to serve it. A bottle can also be chilled in an ice bucket. Place a towel or napkin over it to hold in the cold air.

If you are on a picnic and no ice is available, wrap the bottle in a cold damp cloth and air passing through the wet cloth should cool the bottle within about 30 minutes. Use the towel to hold the wet bottle.

Now the technicalities. Beneath the foil on every bottle of sparkling wine is a wire loop. Unwind it carefully and the wire *muselet* will come off.

Hold the bottle by its base with one hand and place the thumb of the other hand on the cork. This ensures that it won't fly out. The base of the bottle is then gently twisted, left-right, left-right. Remember, it's the bottle that gets twisted. And the best position is to hold the bottle at a 45-degree angle.

For centuries, scholars have argued as to whether or not there should be a loud "pop," with the champagne gushing out of the bottle. Or whether there should be merely a soft moan as the cork eases out.

The jury is no longer out. Count Louis Culpepper, one of the few French Culpeppers to keep his head during the French Revolution, has studied the matter for years.

"It doesn't matter 'ow you do eet," he said. "You paid for eet and you can do w'atever you want."

The only thing to remember is that champagne is under a great deal of pressure and the cork must never be allowed to hit anyone.

24

THE HARD STUFF

WHISKEY

SCOTCH WHISKY

There are two schools of thought on the origin of whisky. One contends that whisky was first made by early Christian monks who settled on the west coast of Scotland.

But I prefer the other theory, that it was distilled by Scottish women folk to warm the blood of their men after a hard day of farming and looking for lost lambs in the mists.

What a bonnie delight it must have been for Hamish Culpepper, having tramped through wet bracken and heather, to spy his wife, Agnes, waiting at home, a glass in her hand. "Y'er probably ready for a wee dram, Hamish," she'd say. "Are you pleased to see me or have ye got something up y're kilt?"

Whisky is the perfect drink with which to entertain a woman. It's easy to serve and there are so many distinctive flavors of whisky that people are now studying them the way they would wine.

Scotch whisky is tasty, and is rich in history. North Americans are the biggest consumers of Scotch whisky.

The earliest account of whisky-making is found in Scottish records of 1494. It must have been a highly-revered brew, for in Scots Gaelic, whiskey is referred to as "uisge beathe," which is taken from the Latin phrase "auga vitae," meaning "water of life."

Many countries have tried to capture the smoky, malt flavor of Scotch, the Japanese have taken everything from peat and water from Scotland to try and make it at home in Nippon. But it can't be done. Methods used in production, the type and character of cereal grains, the type of peat and the quality and character of the spring water employed, all contribute to a distinctive flavor.

Scotch is made mainly from barley. It must be distilled in Scotland, matured in wooden casks in Scotland for at least three years, and, if blended, all whiskies in the blend must be Scotch.

There are about 120 whisky distilleries in Scotland and the value of the whisky maturing in their vats is reckoned to be greater than the reserves held by the Bank of England. Skilled blenders "nose" whisky from many distilleries to create their product from perhaps 40 sources.

Most popular whiskies are blended and served on the rocks (with ice), with or without a little water or soda. The Scots grimace when heathens add mix, such as Sprite, ginger ale and Coke.

Single malt whiskey is made from the produce of only one distillery. Connoisseurs covet "single malts" for their character and pureness of taste. After supper, many prefer them to a brandy. They usually savor the aroma and sip a dram before adding a little water. Single malts can be light, pale and clean like the Lowlander Glenkinchie. Or they can be robust, lingering, smoky and peaty like my favorite, the islay malt, Lagavulin.

ON ME SAINTED GRAN 'MITHER'S GRAVE OI BE GIVEN YE A TERRIBLE, TERRIBLE POUNDIN' BHOY!

IRISH WHISKEY:
Irish whiskey is produced in much the same way as Scotch whisky, but it doesn't have the same smoky quality because of production methods. It is sometimes blended with neutral grain whiskey to produce a lighter-bodied product. (Whisky is spelled without an "e" in Scotland and Canada, but with an "e" in Ireland and the U.S.) **27**

U.S. WHISKEY: Whiskey production in the U.S. began early in the 18th century and the main distillation centers are in Kentucky, Pennsylvania and Indiana. It is made with malt and other grains, usually corn or rye.

CANADIAN WHISKY:
Individual Canadian producers have from the beginning of the 19th century used their own recipes to produce whisky made from mashes composed of combinations of rye, corn, wheat and barley malt. They are usually aged for six years. Canada is known for its rye whisky. Rye possesses the greatest winter hardiness of all small grains.

BOURBON: The main ingredient in bourbon (at least 51 percent) is corn mash, the rest being malt and rye. Bourbon was originally produced in Bourbon County, Kentucky, and in time, "bourbon" was the name given to similar cornmash whiskeys. The liquor is aged in new charred-oak containers.

WHISKEY FAVORITES:

AGGRAVATION
1 oz. Scotch
1 oz. Kahlúa
2 oz. heavy cream
Build in highball glass with cubed ice.

BARRACUDA
¾ oz. bourbon
¼ oz. orgeat
¾ oz. orange juice
Blend with crushed ice. Pour into cocktail glass. Garnish with red cherry.

BOILERMAKER

1 oz. bourbon
cold beer
Serve bourbon in shot glass with beer chaser on the side.

BOURBON HIGHBALL

1¼ oz. bourbon
water, ginger ale, soda, cola or 7-Up.
Build in highball glass. Fill with chosen mixer.

CALIFORNIA LEMONADE

1¼ oz. bourbon
½ oz. sweet-and-sour mix
¼ oz. grenadine
Blend with crushed ice. Pour into sour glass. Garnish with red cherry.

DRY ROB ROY

1¼ oz. Scotch
½ oz. dry vermouth
Build in rock glass with cubed ice. Garnish with green olive.

GODFATHER

¾ oz. Scotch or bourbon
¾ oz. amaretto
Build in rock glass with cubed ice.

JOHN COLLINS

1¼ oz. bourbon
1½ oz. sweet-and-sour mix
7-Up
Build in collins glass with cubed ice. Fill with 7-Up. Garnish with red cherry.

MANHATTAN

1¼ oz. bourbon
½ oz. sweet vermouth
Build in rock glass with cubed ice.
Garnish with red cherry.

OLD ROB

¾ oz. Scotch
¾ oz. sweet vermouth
¼ teaspoon sugar
Dash of bitters
Build in rock glass with cubed ice.

29

PINEAPPLE SOUR
1¼ oz. bourbon
2 oz. pineapple juice
¼ oz. sweet-and-sour mix.
Blend with crushed ice. Pour into cocktail glass.

RATTLESNAKE
1¼ oz. bourbon
dash of anisette
1¼ oz. sweet-and-sour mix.
1 egg white
Blend with crushed ice. Pour into cocktail glass.

ROB ROY
1¼ oz. Scotch
½ oz. sweet vermouth
Build in rock glass with cubed ice. Garnish with red cherry.

RUSTY NAIL
¾ oz. Scotch
¾ oz. Drambuie
Build in rock glass with cubed ice.

STAIRCASE
1 oz. Scotch
¼ oz. dry vermouth
¼ oz. sweet vermouth
¼ oz. Drambuie
Build in rock glass with cubed ice.

YELLOW ROSE
1 oz. bourbon
½ oz. apple brandy
1½ oz. sweet-and-sour mix
Blend with crushed ice. Pour into sour glass. Garnish with red cherry.

GIN

A good gin is as dry as Oscar Wilde's wit and as smooth as English silk. It's usually served in cocktails such as the martini and gimlet and in long drinks such as the Tom Collins and gin and tonic.

It's a great drink to serve if you're having a hard time getting the conversation with your dinner date to flow, because there are so many neat things you can tell her about gin.

The big British gin companies, such as Beefeater, Tanqueray, Booth's and Gordon's, all have their secret recipes and won't tell you a darn thing about them.

I once had lunch in the Wig and Pen Club in Fleet Street with John Tanqueray, whose grandpa founded the London-based Tanqueray gin company. And he was most guarded when I suggested he tell me what the heck was in the family brew. "Our family formula is kept under triple lock in a ledger that we refer to reverently as our Bible," he said with a stiff upper lip. "You couldn't pry the secret from me even if you pulled out my fingernails."

What everyone knows is that gin is distilled from purified spirits usually obtained from a grain mash. Juniper berries provide the main flavoring. **31**

But no one knows the exact combination of lemon, angelica, orris, licorice roots, cassia bark, coriander, caraway, cardamom, anise and fennel that might be used to flavor a particular brand.

Holland's Franciscus Sylvius, a 17th-century professor at the University of Leiden, is credited with inventing gin after distilling the juniper berry with spirits to produce an inexpensive medicine.

The French name for the juniper berry, *genievre*, was changed to *genever* by the Dutch. And the good old Brits decided gin was good enough. Soldiers fighting in the Low Countries in the early 18th century took it back to England and handed their contemporaries a social problem. Gin could be produced so inexpensively that it was consumed in abundance and public drunkenness became a problem. Gin shops would advertise: "Drunk for a penny, dead drunk for tuppence and clean straw for nothing."

Later, when the Union Jack flew over India and what was then Ceylon, guardians of the British Empire took quinine to ward off tropical diseases – and found it tasted better with gin.

Gin is the base of many good drinks. Work your way through the ones that follow and remember what John Fletcher said:

Drink today, and down all sorrow,
32 *You shall perhaps not do it tomorrow.*

GIN FAVORITES:

APPLESAUCE
1 oz. gin
¾ oz. apple brandy
¾ tsp. grenadine
1 oz. sweet-and-sour mix
1 oz. orange juice
Blend with crushed ice. Pour into sour glass. Garnish with red cherry.

BERMUDA COCKTAIL
1 oz. gin
¾ oz. peach brandy
¼ oz. grenadine
¼ oz. orange juice
Blend with crushed ice. Pour into cocktail glass.

DEPTH CHARGE
1 oz. gin
½ oz. triple sec
2 dashes of anisette (float)
Blend with crushed ice. Pour into wine glass. Float anisette.

FRENCH 75
1¼ oz. gin
1 oz. sweet-and-sour mix
½ oz. soda
champagne
Build in collins glass with crushed ice. Fill with champagne.

GIMLET
1¼ oz. gin
½ oz. Rose's Lime Juice
Blend with crushed ice. Serve in wine glass. Garnish with green cherry.

GIN PUNCH
1 oz. gin
1 oz. coconut milk
½ oz. Cherry Heering
1 oz. orange juice
1 oz. pineapple juice.
Blend with crushed ice. Pour into collins glass. Garnish with orange slice and red cherry.

GIN ROSE
1¼ oz. gin
1¼ oz. sweet-and-sour mix
¼ oz. grenadine
Blend with crushed ice. Pour into sour glass. Garnish with red cherry.

33

GRAND SLAM

1 oz. gin
¼ oz. Grand Marnier
1 oz. orange juice
¾ tsp. grenadine
Blend with crushed ice. Pour into sour glass.
Garnish with red cherry.

HONOLULU COCKTAIL

1¼ oz. gin
1 oz. orange juice
1 oz. pineapple juice
½ oz. sweet-and-sour mix
Blend with crushed ice. Pour into bucket glass.
Garnish with red cherry.

ORANGE GIMLET

1¼ oz. gin
¼ oz. Rose's Lime Juice
½ oz. orange juice
¼ oz. fresh lime juice
Blend with crushed ice. Pour into wine glass.
Garnish with orange slice and green cherry.

PINEAPPLE MINT COOLER

¾ oz. gin
¾ oz. green crème de menthe
2 oz. pineapple juice
Build in collins glass with crushed ice.

RED DERBY

1 oz. gin
½ oz apricot brandy
½ oz. fresh lemon juice
¾ tsp. grenadine
Blend with crushed ice. Pour into
sour glass. Garnish with red
cherry.

SINGAPORE SLING

1¼ oz. gin
1¾ oz sweet-and-sour mix
½ oz. soda
¼ oz. cherry brandy (float)
¼ oz. grenadine (float)
Build in collins glass with crushed
ice. Add soda. Float brandy and grenadine.
Cherry garnish.

TOM COLLINS

1¼ oz. gin
1½ oz. sweet-and-sour mix
7-Up
34 Build in collins glass with cubed ice.
Fill with 7-Up. Garnish with red cherry.

RUM

RUM

Pirate ships . . .
The Caribbean . . .
And buried treasure . . .

No swashbuckling bachelor should be without a bottle of rum in his munitions chest. It's the stuff of romance.

Robert Louis Stevenson wrote it into folklore in 1883 when he penned *Treasure Island* and included the pirate chant:

Fifteen men on the dead man's chest
  Yo-ho-ho, and a bottle of rum!
Drink and the devil had done for the rest –
  Yo-ho-ho, and a bottle of rum!

Rum, a liquor made from sugar cane products, was the major liquid distilled during the early history of North America.

New England rum has been made in the U.S. for more than 300 years, In fur-trapping Canada, it was possible to get a bottle of Hudson's Bay rum at just about any of the trading company's far-flung forts.

One of the most called-for summer drinks today is a Mai Tai, which mixes 1½ ounces of rum with 1½ ounce of crème de almond. It's served over ice with pineapple juice, garnished with a pineapple stick and a cherry.

But who hasn't, at some point in their life, enjoyed a hot-buttered rum? There's nothing on a stormy night that warms a person faster than an ample shot of rum in boiling water, with a pat of butter floating on top.

Rums originated in the West Indies and were first mentioned in records from Barbados in the middle of the 17th-century. Today, we are used to the light-bodied rums typified by those of Cuba and Puerto Rico, and the heavier and fuller-favored rums of Jamaica, Barbados and Demerara, Guyana.

Oak aging and caramel help give some rums their golden color.

As a man-about-town, it's of course worth knowing that rum featured in the slave commerce of the American colonies. In triangular trade, slaves were brought from Africa and traded to the West Indies for molasses. the molasses was taken to New England and made into rum, which was then traded in Africa for more slaves.

If you are serving your date a rum drink, you might want to throw in some interesting trivia. The British navy served rum to their men until 1970, but Sir Winston Churchill once took a swipe at the Senior Service and its customs. "Don't talk to me about naval tradition," he declared. "It's nothing but rum, sodomy and the lash."

It sounds like one of the many brilliant sayings that seemed to come off the top of his head. But it is worth noting that a naval catch-phrase from the 19th-century ran: "Ashore it's wine, women and song, aboard, it's rum, bum and concertina."

And that nicely gets the conversation round to a man's need for sex.

RUM FAVORITES:

BACARDI COCKTAIL
1¼ oz. Bacardi rum
1½ oz. sweet-and-sour mix
¼ oz. grenadine
Blend with crushed ice. Pour into sour glass.
Garnish with red cherry.

BANANA DAIQUIRI
1¼ oz. rum
1¼ oz. sweet-and-sour mix
¼ oz. banana liqueur
1 banana
Blended with crushed ice. Pour into sour glass.

BETWEEN THE SHEETS
¾ oz. rum
¾ oz. brandy
½ oz. Triple Sec
1½ oz. sweet-and-sour mix
Blend with crushed ice. Pour into cocktail glass.

CUBA LIBRE
1¼ oz. rum
cola
Build in highball
glass with cubed
ice. Fill with cola.
Garnish with
squeeze of lime.

DAIQUIRI
1¼ oz. rum
1½ oz. sweet-and-
sour mix
Blend with crushed ice.
Pour into sour glass. Garnish with red cherry.

GOLDEN COLADA
1 oz. rum
½ oz. Galliano
1 oz. coconut milk
¾ oz. pineapple juice
¾ oz. orange juice
¼ oz. Curaçao
Blend with crushed ice. Pour into bucket glass.
Garnish with red cherry and orange slice.

ISLANDER

1¼ oz. rum
1 oz. papaya juice
1 oz. pineapple juice
1 oz. coconut juice
Blend with crushed ice. Pour into bucket glass. Garnish with red cherry.

JAMAICAN SHAKE

1¼ oz. rum
1 scoop vanilla ice cream
1 oz. pineapple juice
¼ oz. grenadine
1 oz. heavy cream
Blend with crushed ice. Pour into bucket glass.

MAI TAI

1 oz. light rum
1 oz. Myer's rum
¾ oz. orange juice
¾ oz. pineapple juice
¾ oz. sweet-and-sour mix
¼ oz. grenadine
½ oz. orgeat
¼ oz. orange Curaçao
Build in bucket glass with crushed ice. Garnish with red cherry and orange slice.

PIÑA COLADA

1¼ oz. rum
¾ oz. orange juice
1 oz. coconut milk
¾ oz. pineapple juice
¼ oz. Curaçao
Blend with crushed ice. Pour into bucket glass. Garnish with red cherry and orange slice.

PLANTER'S PUNCH

1¼ oz. Myer's rum
¾ oz. orange juice
¾ oz. pineapple juice
¼ oz. Rose's Lime Juice
¼ oz. grenadine
Build in bucket glass with crushed ice. Garnish with red cherry and orange slice.

RUM NOG
1¼ oz. rum
1 egg
4 oz. milk
1 tsp. sugar
dash of vanilla
Blend with crushed ice. Pour into wine glass.
Garnish with sprinkle of nutmeg.

SCORPION
1¼ oz. rum
¾ oz. brandy
½ oz. orgeat
2 oz. orange juice
1½ oz. sweet-and-sour mix
Build in bucket glass with crushed ice. Garnish
with red cherry and orange slice.

TANGERINE
1¼ oz rum
¼ oz. Curaçao
2 oz. pineapple juice
¼ oz. grenadine
1 egg white
Blend with crushed ice. Pour into bucket glass.
Garnish with red cherry and orange slice.

ZOMBIE
¾ oz. light rum
¾ oz Myer's rum
¾ oz. Don Q Gold Rum
¾ oz. sweet-and-sour mix
¾ oz. orange juice
¾ oz. pineapple juice
½ oz. grenadine
¼ oz. 151-proof rum (float)
Build in bucket glass with
crushed ice. Float rum. Garnish
with red cherry and
40 orange slice.

VODKA

VODKA

Illyvanovich Culpepper, a 14th-century cossack, wrote Culpepper clans around the world extolling the merits of vodka.

No one would take him seriously because they reckoned, rightly, that the word vodka was derived from voda (Russian for water).

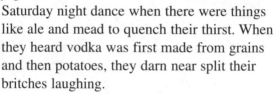

They couldn't imagine knocking back great jugs of water at the Saturday night dance when there were things like ale and mead to quench their thirst. When they heard vodka was first made from grains and then potatoes, they darn near split their britches laughing.

Five centuries later, just after the Second World War to be more exact, vodka took off in North America and Europe when it was discovered to be pretty well tasteless and high in alcohol content. Bartenders decided it was the perfect base on which to build a cocktail. And cereal grains became the base for vodka.

The Russians, Poles and peoples of the Balkan states went on drinking their lower-proof vodka, unmixed and chilled. But in London, Paris and New York, they quickly invented the Screwdriver (vodka and orange juice); the Bloody Mary (vodka and tomato juice) and they even substituted it for gin in a martini.

Illyvanovich Culpepper would have laughed in their faces and said: "You could have had Smirnoff, Gordon's, Stolichnaya and Absolute 500 years ago, you jugheads."

VODKA FAVORITES:

BLACK RUSSIAN
¾ oz. vodka
¾ oz. Kahlúa
Build in rock glass with cubed ice.

BLOODY MARY
1¼ oz. vodka
3 oz. tomato juice
2 dashes of Worcestershire sauce
dash of Tabasco sauce
black pepper
celery salt
salt
¾ teaspoon fresh lime juice
Build in collins glass with cubed ice. Squeeze in
lime juice.

CHI-CHI
1¼ oz. vodka
2 oz. pineapple juice
2 oz. coconut milk
¼ oz. orange Curaçao
Blend with crushed ice. Pour into collins glass.

FLYING GRASSHOPPER
¾ oz. vodka
¾ oz. green crème de menthe
¾ oz. white crème de cacao
Build in rock glass with cubed ice.

GREYHOUND
1¼ oz. vodka
grapefruit juice
Build in collins glass with cubed ice. Fill with
grapefruit juice.

RED BIRD
1 oz. vodka
3 oz. tomato juice
cold beer
Build in collins glass with cubed ice.
Fill with beer.

43

SALTY DOG
1¼ oz. vodka
grapefruit juice
Build in salt-rimmed collins glass with cubed ice. Fill with grapefruit juice.

SCREWDRIVER
1-1/4 oz. vodka
orange juice
Build in collins glass with cubed ice. Fill with orange juice.

SKIP AND GO NAKED
1¼ oz. vodka
1¼ oz. sweet-and- sour mix
cold beer
Build in collins glass with cubed ice. Fill with beer.

SWEET BANANA
1 oz. vodka
½ oz crème de banana
½ fresh banana
1 oz. sweet-and-sour mix
Blend with crushed ice. Pour into sour glass.

VODKA BLUE
1¼ oz. vodka
1½ oz. orange juice
1½ oz. pineapple juice
1 oz. sweet-and-sour mix
½ oz. blue Curaçao
Blend with crushed ice.
Pour into collins glass.
Garnish with red cherry.

VODKA GIMLET
1½ oz. vodka
½ oz. Rose's Lime Juice
Blend with crushed ice.
Garnish with green cherry.

VODKA SLING
1¼ oz. vodka
1¾ oz. sweet-and-sour mix
½ oz. soda
¼ oz. cherry brandy (float)
¼ oz. grenadine (float)
Build in collins glass with crushed ice. Add soda. Float brandy and grenadine.
44 Garnish with red cherry.

WHITE RUSSIAN

¾ oz. vodka

¾ oz. Kahlúa

½ oz. heavy cream

Build in rock glass with cubed ice.

YELLOW-FELLOW

1 oz. vodka

½ oz. Cointreau

2 oz. pineapple juice

Blend with crushed ice. Pour into cocktail glass

MARTINI.

"SEX IS GOOD.
BUT NOT AS
GOOD AS A
DRY MARTINI!"

Lady Cynthia Culpepper

MARTINI

To the embarrassment of the British branch of the Culpepper family, Lady Cynthia Culpepper had an affair with a stable boy at Ascot race track. The family tried to hush the matter up, but the lad sold his story to a Sunday tabloid for £2,000 and the dreadful matter entered the public domain.

All would have been lost had Lady Cynthia not had the good sense to put her rather passionate appetite in perspective.

When asked to comment, she told a reporter: "Sex is good, but not as good as a dry martini!"

The newspaper ran a front page photo of her winking and sipping a martini, and several gin companies tried to sponsor her next safari.

To some, the martini is the king of drinks. It's a powerful, special-occasion drink. It stands on its own, an Everest surrounded by foothills.

It was no accident that Ernest Hemingway had Colonel Cantwell order a martini for himself and his 19-year-old sweetheart, Renata, in *Across the River and Into the Trees*. It was a stiff one – we're talking about the drink – 15 parts gin to one part vermouth, the perfect catalyst to the goings on.

The only mistake he might have made, in some people's opinion, is that he asked for any vermouth at all. They like it left out entirely.

Sir Winston Churchill said the best martinis are prepared with a mere glance at the vermouth bottle. In his famous gravel voice, the greatest statesman who ever lived once declared: "The best martini is made with gin, gin and gin!"

While most of the martini aficionados I know like gin, some people do call for a vodka martini.

You'd better have supper well on the way before you fool with a stiff martini, and a torch-light procession marches down your throat.

But having said that, there can be no better libation to bring two people together. Making a martini while being watched by someone adds an immediate element of complicity. Expectations soar, never to be disappointed. Nothing is more certain to deliver. And there's that special ritual when you feed one another the olives at the bottom of the glass. Incredibly symbolic. The giving of the inner self. Peace at last.

There are a couple of tricks to making sure a martini is topnotch. The first is to throw a couple of glasses in the freezer as soon as you think about martinis. If you know that's what you are going to drink, or even suspect you might, put the gin or vodka bottle in there as well for a spell. If caught totally off guard, you  can place the glass rim downwards in the ice tray while you go to work.

Next, decide whether you are going to serve the martini straight up (without ice) or on the rocks (with ice).

Serious martini drinkers call for a straight up martini, knowing that the ice is going to melt and dilute the libation. But if pushed for time, even a serious martini drinker will take one on the rocks rather than miss out altogether.

If your girl friend calls for a martini on the rocks, simply grab a handful of ice, throw it into a martini glass, or whatever you serve your drinks in, and splash gin or vodka over it. A touch of vermouth can go in if you like. Serve with a stirrer and an olive or two.

The serious dry martini drinker will stir 1/2 an ounce of dry vermouth in a shaker and then either dump out the vermouth once the ice has taken on its taste or leave it in. Next, two ounces of gin or vodka are added and they are stirred once or twice. No more. Never bruise the gin.

A strainer is placed over the mixing glass and the martini is poured into the glass from the freezer. Always pour over the prongs of the strainer. Traditionally, an olive or two are served in the martini. But if you like it very dry, a twist of lemon works wonders.

If you know you are going to have a couple of martinis, it's best to mix a batch before your guest arrives and let it chill in the freezer. Lady Cynthia always did.

EXTRA DRY MARTINI: Use only a drop or two of vermouth.

BONE DRY MARTINI: Use straight gin or vodka.

INCREDIBLY DRY MARTINI: Add a drop of Scotch to dry out your martini.

GIBSON: A martini that is garnished with a cocktail onion instead of an olive. **49**

TEQUILA

TEQUILA

Some of the world's great drinks are made with tequila, a potent brew made in Mexico from the agave plant. Where would civilization be today without the Margarita, the Mexican Screw

(a Screwdriver made with tequila instead of vodka), the Tequila Sunrise and the Tequila Sunset?

Tequila contains about 40-50 percent alcohol (80-100 U.S. proof) and was developed soon after the Spaniards introduced distillation to Mexico.

When it matures, the pineapple-shaped agave base fills with sweet sap, or aqua miel (honey water). This juice is used to make either clear or amber-colored tequila.

Oak vats are sometimes used to mellow the brew and amber tequila, called "gold," takes its color from this aging wood.

If you have a Mexican theme party, you will certainly want to impress your date with a flight of Margaritas, which are made with lime juice and served in a glass rimmed with salt.

But such an evening would be incomplete if you didn't "go Mexican" and follow the time-honored custom of knocking back some straight tequila.

The ritual is simple:
- Salt is sprinkled in the web of the hand between the thumb and forefinger.
- A lime wedge is held by the thumb and forefinger
- The tequila shot is held in the other hand
- Lick the salt, do the shotand then bite the lime.
  Ole!

51

TEQUILA FAVORITES:

BANANA PANTHER
1¼ oz. tequila
2 sweet-and-sour mix
1 banana
Blend with crushed ice. Pour into sour glass.

DECEIVER
1 oz. tequila
½ oz. Galliano
Build in rock glass with cubed ice.

FREDDY FUDD
1¼ oz. tequila
2 ½ oz. orange juice
½ oz. Galliano
Build in collins glass with cubed ice.

MARGARITA
1¼ oz. tequila
½ oz. Triple Sec
¼-½ oz. Rose's
  Lime Juice
1½ oz. sweet-and-
  sour mix
Blend with crushed
ice. Serve in cock-
tail glass rimmed
with salt.

MEXICAN ALMOND
¾ oz. tequila
¾ oz. amaretto
Build in rock glass with cubed ice.

MEXICAN MELON
1¼ oz. tequila
½ cup diced, seeded watermelon
1 oz. sweet-and-sour mix
¼ oz. crème de cassis
Blend with crushed ice. Pout into sour glass.
Garnish with lemon twist.

PANTHER
1 oz. tequila
½ oz. sweet-and-sour mix
Build in rock glass with cubed ice.

TEQUICHI

1¼ oz. tequila
1½ oz. coconut milk
¾ oz. pineapple juice
Blend with crushed ice. Pour into sour glass.

TEQUILA BLOODY MARY

1¼oz. tequila
1½ oz. tomato juice
1½ oz. beef bouillon
¾ teaspoon fresh lime juice
2 dashes of Worcestershire sauce
dash of Tabasco sauce
black pepper
celery salt
salt
Build in collins glass with cubed ice. Garnish
with lime wedge.

TEQUILA DRIVER

1¼ oz. tequila
orange juice
Build in collins glass with cubed ice. Fill with
orange juice.

TEQUILA PUNCH

1¼ oz. tequila
1½ oz. pineapple
  juice
1½ oz. orange
  juice
½ oz. sweet-
  and-sour mix
grenadine
  (float)
Blend with
crushed ice. Pour into
sour glass. Float grena-
dine.

KNOCK-OUT
PUNCH, CHAMP!

TEQUILA SLING

1 oz. tequila
2 oz. sweet-and-sour mix
½ oz. soda
¼ oz. cherry brandy
¼ oz. sloe gin
Build in collins glass with crushed ice. Garnish
with red cherry and orange juice.

TEQUILA SUNRISE
1¼ oz. tequila
1-1.2 oz. orange juice
½ oz. sweet-and-sour mix
Dash of grenadine (float)
¼ oz. crème de cassis (float)
Build in collins glass with crushed ice. Or blend with crushed ice and pour into collins glass. Float grenadine and crème de cassis. Garnish with red cherry.

TEQUILA SUNSET
1¼ oz. tequila
¾ oz. orange juice
¾ oz. pineapple juice
¾ oz. coconut milk
¾ oz. sloe gin (float)
Build in collins glass with crushed ice. Float sloe gin.

COCKTAILS

THE COCKTAIL

TELL THIS GUY HE'S GOT HIS FACTS WRONG!

For many years, people, including learned university professors, believed that the word "cocktail" was derived somehow from using a bird's plumage to stir a drink.

Nothing could be further from the truth. But it wasn't until the diary of the most famous frontier scout of them all was found that the mystery was solved.

Tonto Culpepper did invaluable tracking work for the American Army in it's frequent scrimmages, at the beginning of the 1800s, with Mexico's King Axolotl VIII.

Sensing the North American Free Trade Agreement was less than a couple of hundred years away, the King and the American general leading the army in the south decided to bury the sabre.

They got together at the King's pad and Tonto remembers the King clapping his hands and calling for a drink.

Into the room came a young, dusky maiden of such tremendous beauty that the General had to pinch himself to make sure he wasn't hallucinating.

According to Tonto, the woman carried a golden chalice set with jewels as big as the Americans' eyeballs. In the cup was a special drink she had invented.

Suddenly, a pregnant hush fell over the gathering as it flashed on everyone at the same time that one of the two great men was going to have to sup first and the other was going to be peeved.

But the woman was a match for the situation, as all great ladies are. She smiled a smile as big as the desert, bent low like a palm in the wind and then supped the beverage herself.

A diplomatic incident avoided, the King and the general sorted things out. But as he was leaving, the general politely asked who the young lady was.

The King, who had absolutely no idea but sensed a chance to impress, replied: "That was my daughter, Coctel."

"No kidding," said the general. "I will make sure that her name is honored forever by my army."

Well, word of the maiden's beauty spread amongst the troopers and the story of the general's encounter was mistold so often that the soldiers ultimely raised their glasses to "Cocktail" instead of "Coctel."

"An easy mistake," wrote Tonto, who later drowned on one of the first raft runs in the Grand Canyon. A camera crew making an IMAX movie found his washed-up diary in 1984, buried in the sand.

But the word "Cocktail" quickly became synonymous with a drink and by 1806, an American magazine called The Balance reported: "Cocktail is a stimulating liquor, composed of spirits of any kind, sugar, water, and bitters – it is vulgarly called bittered sling and is supposed to be an excellent electioneering potion."

The best cocktails have been invented and reinvented many times. But Harry Craddock, of the Savoy Hotel in London, who published The Savoy Cocktail Book in 1930, said there is only one way to drink a cocktail. "Quickly," he said, "while it is still laughing at you."

COCKTAIL FAVORITES

ACAPULCO GOLD
¾ oz. white rum
½ oz. Cointreau
pineapple juice
lemon juice

ALEXANDER
¾ oz. brandy
½ oz. crème de cacao
cream

BANANA BOAT
⅔ oz. vodka
⅓ oz. crème de banana
orange juice
grenadine

BANANA SANDWICH
¾ oz crème de banana
½ oz. crème de cacao
cream

BARTENDER'S ROOTBEER
1 oz. Kahlúa
¼ oz. Galliano
soda
coke

BLONDE BOMBSHELL
⅔ oz crème de banana
⅓ oz. tequila
milk

BLUE MONDAY
¾ oz. vodka
½ oz. Parfait Amour
7-Up

BOMBAY SLING
⅓ oz rye
⅓ oz. gin
⅓ oz. sherry
lemon juice
orange juice

BROWN COW
1 oz. Kahlúa
milk

CAESAR

1¼ oz. vodka
3 oz. clamato juice
2 dashes of
  Worcestershire sauce
dash of Tabasco
  sauce
black pepper
celery salt
salt
¾ tsp. fresh lime juice
Build in collins glass with
cubed ice. Squeeze in lime
juice. Garnish with celery.

CREAMSICLE

1 oz. pear liqueur
milk
orange juice

DIRTY MOTHER

¾ oz. tequila
½ oz. Kahlúa
cream

DUBONNET COCKTAIL

¾ oz. Dubonnet
½ oz. gin
lemon slice

FIFTH AVENUE

¾ oz. apricot brandy
½ oz. crème de cacao cream

FUZZY NAVEL

1 oz. peach schnapps
orange juice

GOLDEN CADILLAC

¾ oz. crème de cacao
½ oz. Galliano cream
cream

GRASSHOPPER

¾ oz. crème de menthe
½ oz. crème de Cacao
cream

HARVEY WALLBANGER

1 oz. vodka
¼ oz. Galliano
60   orange juice

KAHLÚA COOLER
⅓ oz Kahlúa
⅓ oz white rum
⅓ oz. gin
coke
lime juice

LONG ISLAND ICED TEA
¼ oz. vodka
¼ oz. gin
½ oz. rum
½ oz. apricot brandy
lemon juice
coke

MELON BALL
1 oz. melon liqueur
lime juice
7-Up

MONKEY'S LUNCH
¾ oz. crème de Banana
½ oz. Kahlúa
cream

NEW YORK COCKTAIL
1 oz. rye
lemon juice
grenadine

PARALYZER
½ oz. of your
   favorite white
   liquor
½ oz. Kahlúa
milk
coke

PIÑA COLADA
1½ oz. rum
coconut syrup
cream

PINK LADY
1¼ oz. gin
grenadine
cream

PLAYBOY
⅔ oz. white rum
⅓ oz. Kahlúa
pineapple juice
coke

61

RUSTY NAIL
1 oz. Scotch
½ oz. Drambuie

SCARLET O 'HARA
1 oz. Southern Comfort
lime juice
grenadine
Garnish with a cherry.

SCORPION
¾ oz. rum
¼ oz. amaretto
¼ oz. brandy
orange juice
lemon juice

SCREAMING ORGASM
¼ oz. vodka
¼ oz. amaretto
¼ oz. Kahlúa
¼ oz. Bailey's Irish Cream

SEX IN THE POOL
¼ oz. rum
¼ oz. wild berry schnapps
orange juice
cranberry juice

SEX ON THE BEACH
¼ oz. vodka
¼ peach schnapps
orange juice
cranberry juice

SIDE CAR
⅔ oz. brandy
⅓ oz. Cointreau
lemon juice

VELVET HAMMER
¾ oz. Cointreau
½ oz Kahlúa
cream

WHITE RUSSIAN
¾ oz. vodka
½ oz. Kahlúa
cream

SHOOTERS

SHOOTERS

AFTER 8
⅓ Kahlúa
⅓ crème de menthe
⅓ Bailey's

ALABAMA SLAMMER
⅓ amaretto
⅓ Grand Marnier
⅓ Southern Comfort

B-52
⅓ Kahlúa
⅓ Bailey's
1⅓ Grand Marnier

B-53
¼ Kahlúa
¼ Baileys
¼ Grand Marnier
¼ tequila

B-57
⅓ Kahlúa
⅓ Triple Sec
⅓ Sambuca

BACHELOR'S SURPRISE
⅓ Kahlúa
⅓ amaretto
⅓ Southern Comfort
Shake, strain and
serve.

Bazooka Joe
⅓ Bailey's
⅓ Parfait Amour
⅓ crème de
  banana
Shake,
strain and
serve.

BEAM ME UP SCOTTIE
⅓ Kahlúa
⅓ Bailey's
⅓ banana liqueur

BETHLEHEM BURNER

½ Grand Marnier
½ sambuca
pinch of nutmeg
pinch of cinnamon
matches
small sidecart of cream

Use a large glass, preferably a martini glass. Layer the GM and sambuca, light, toss in the nutmeg and sprinkle cinnamon from 12 inches above (brings the flame up high), finish off with the cream (to put out the fire).

BLACK CAT

½ Kahlúa
½ vodka

BLEEDING BRAIN

½ peach schnapps
½ Bailey's
few drops of grenadine

BLOW JOB

⅓ Kahlúa
⅓ banana liqueur
⅓ Bailey's
whipped cream

BLUE-EYED BLONDE

⅓ banana liqueur
⅓ Parfait Amour
⅓ advocaat

BRAIN HEMORRHAGE

⅓ peach schnapps
⅓ Bailey's
3 drops of grena
  dine

Layer the Bailey's on top of the peach schnapps and drip in the grenadine to create the hemorrhage.

CANDY CANE

½ crème de menthe
½ peppermint schnapps
few drops of grenadine

CHANEL 69
⅓ banana liqueur
⅓ advocaat
⅓ Bailey's

CHINA WHITE
½ crème de cacao (white)
½ Bailey's
pinch of cinnamon
Can layer, but is very nice shaken over ice and strained. Sprinkle cinnamon on top.

CHOCOLATE CHIP
⅓ swiss chocolate almond
⅓ Bailey's
⅓ peppermint schnapps

CHOCOLATE SUNDAE
⅓ Kahlúa
⅓ Bailey's
⅓ white crème de cacao
whipped cream

CLEAVAGE
½ rootbeer
    schnapps
½ sambuca

COMA
⅓ Kahlúa
⅓ anisette
⅓ Grand Marnier

COOL KISS
½ southern comfort
½ peppermint schnapps

COSMIC COWBOY
⅓ Yukon Jack
⅓ Jack Daniels
⅓ Southern Comfort

CREAMY NUTS
⅓ Kahlúa
⅓ Bailey's
⅓ Malibu

DOUBLE JACK
½ Jack Daniels
½ Yukon Jack

EARTHQUAKE

⅓ anisette
⅓ amaretto
⅓ South Comfort

ELECTRIC BANANA

½ tequila
½ banana liqueur

ELECTRIC POPSICLE

⅓ vodka
⅓ Parfait Amour
⅓ lime juice
Shake strain, and serve.

GHOST BUSTER

½ parfait amour
½ vodka
drop of cream

GOLD RUSH

½ Southern Comfort
½ Yukon Jack

GOOD & PLENTY

½ sambuca
½ tequila

GORILLA SNOT

¾ melon liqueur
¼ advocaat
3 drops of grenadine
Drip the advocaat into the
melon liqueur, and top
with grenadine.

GREEN MONKEY

½ crème de menthe
½ banana liqueur

HARD ON

⅓ Kahlúa
⅓ anisette
⅓ Bailey's

INNOCENT EYES

⅓ Kahlúa
⅓ sambuca
⅓ Bailey's

IRISH MONKEY
½ banana liqueur
½ Bailey's

JELL-O SHOOTER
1 pkg. Jell-o mix
vodka, tequila, white rum (your favorite)
Follow directions on Jell-o mix replacing water
with alcohol. Pour in shooter glasses or pill bottles. Throw them in the fridge (if you're rushed
for time, throw them in the freezer). Wait until
the gelatin sets and serve.

JELLY BEAN
½ tequila
½ anisette
Few drops of grenadine

KAMAKAZE
⅓ vodka
⅓ Triple Sec
⅓ lime juice

KNOB GOBBLER
½ Bailey's
½ butter ripple schnapps
Shake, strain and serve.

PIECE OF ASS
⅓ Southern Comfort
⅓ amaretto
⅓ lime juice
Shake, strain and serve.

SEX ON THE BEACH
⅓ Bailey's
⅓ crème de banana
⅓ sambuca

SEX ON THE POOL TABLE
⅓ Bailey's
⅓ crème de menthe (green)
⅓ sambuca
Shake, strain and serve.

SICILIAN KISS
½ Southern Comfort
½ amaretto

SLIPPERY NIPPLE
½ Bailey's
½ sambuca
Shake, strain and serve.

NON-ALCOHOLIC

NO THANK YOU, I'LL HAVE A JUICE

Incredible as it may seem, there are people in the world who don't drink. Many a man would give up trying to impress and write the evening off on discovering his dinner date didn't like a tipple.

But not you. You bend in the wind like a tree, get your breath back and turn to this page immediately. Perhaps even leave some kind of bookmark here so that you will be able to find it in cases of emergency. A wine label works well.

While you are looking up some of the nonalcoholic drink recipes that follow, serve a juice or some other type of soft drink. You've probably got some mix on hand that will do just fine when poured over ice. Then you say something like: "I hardly ever touch the stuff myself. I believe Thoreau was right when he wrote that "water is the only drink for a wise man."

If that gets a smile, go for the old one-two combination and add: "I remember reading in the *Koran* that, there is a devil in every berry of the grape."

You'll have to play it by ear after that, but if your dinner partner goes on about how bad booze is, you might throw in: "You're right of course. Bacchus has drowned more men that Neptune. And it was Seneca who said that 'drunkenness is nothing but voluntary madness.' He should know. He played left wing for the Athens' soccer team, alongside Pele Culpepper."

In most cases, you will be over the hurdle by now and your new-found-hero status will let you suggest a fireside massage after supper.

In the odd case, a final upper cut of sincerity may be needed. Valentino Culpepper, who starred in several silent movies, would get down on one knee, ring in his hands and take a short line from Shakespeare's Othello. "O God," he'd say. "That men should put an enemy in their mouths to steal away their brains! That we should, with joy, pleasance, revel, and applause, transform ourselves into beasts!" Valentino Culpepper never failed to score.

Any creative bachelor can have fun concocting a nonalcoholic punch. Flatter your date and name it after her.

Begin by finding a suitable container for your brew. Most bachelors don't have punch bowls, as they rightly figure they will be acquired as wedding presents. But many other things will suffice. For instance, it's easy to get your hands on a vase. Any vase will do, although crystal is a bonus. Fill it up, throw in a couple of cherries and enjoy watching people try to fish them from the bottom. A ladle of a suitable length and girth should be handy.

In deciding on your ingredients, it's important to remember that your punch must neither be too sweet nor too bitter. Good bases include pineapple, orange, strawberry and apple juices.

Consideration should also be given to color. Nobody likes a murky punch, that often comes from using such things as dairy products. Grenadine and lemonade work well and add a nice touch of color. Pink lemonade is especially good. Remember that old line: Pink to make the girls wink.

71

Ginger ale, Sprite or 7-Up add a pleasing, fresh touch that comes from carbonation. Use diet versions of the drinks and you'll make a lot of friends. Don't use a cola. Colas don't work in punches.

Cut up some fresh fruit and add for decoration. Be bold. Women like men with innovative minds.

NONALCOHOLIC FAVORITES:

BASIC TEA PUNCH
2 cups strong hot tea
6 cups of your favorite fruit juice
2 cups ginger ale or
    soda water
Combine just
before serving
and sweeten to
taste with sugar
or syrup, etc.
Pour over a
block of ice in
a punch bowl
and let chill.

BLACK AND TAN
cola
milk
In a tall glass, place 1 or 2 ice cubes, fill ⅔ full with cola. Fill up with milk. Stir and serve.

ORANGEADE (Serves 4-6)
juice of 5 oranges
juice of 1 lemon
½ cup sugar syrup
1 quart water
Combine in pitcher and chill. Pour over ice cubes in tall glasses. Garnish with fruit or mint as desired.

PINK PEARL
1 cup grapefruit juice
2 teaspoons lemon juice
1 or 2 teaspoons grenadine
1 or 2 egg whites
Shake with crushed ice and strain into cocktail glass.

ROSEY SQUASH

½ lemon
1 tablespoon grenadine
soda water

In a tumbler place ice cubes, add the juice of ½ lemon, grenadine and fill with soda water.

SUMMER FIZZ (Serves 8)

12 sprigs mint
½ cup lemon juice
1 cup currant jelly
1 cup hot water
1 cup cold water
3 cups orange juice
1 bottle ginger ale

Crush mint in a bowl and add boiling water and currant jelly. When jelly is melted, add cold water. Strain, when cold, into punch bowl. Add fruit juices and block of ice. Just before serving, pour in ginger ale and decorate with mint.

TEMPERANCE PUNCH

½ lb. powdered sugar
1 quart cold tea
2 cups lemon juice
1 quart soda
2 quarts white grape juice

Combine all ingredients in punch bowl with a block of ice. Stir and decorate with fruit as desired.

PINEAPPLE ICED TEA

3 oz. Nestlé liquid iced tea
3 oz. pineapple juice
Pour over ice.

PINEAPPLE STRAWBERRY ICED TEA

2½ oz. Nestlé liquid iced tea
3 oz. pineapple juice
½ oz. strawberry syrup
Blend and pour over ice.

FRESH PINEAPPLE ICED TEA

1 oz. pineapple
5 oz. Nestlé liquid iced tea
2 large ice cubes

In a medium-sized pitcher, blend all together and pour in glass. Garnish with pineapple wedge; add a splash of vodka for a change or blend in a couple of strawberries.

THE WORLD'S TEN BEST PICKUP LINES

THE WORLD'S TEN BEST PICKUP LINES

James "Bond" Culpepper, no stranger to stirred martinis and 30 extra pounds, was once playing the tables in Monaco when he thought he'd won the admiration of a young starlet standing next to him. "I'm stepping outside to catch some fresh air," he said. "Care to join me in a drink?"

"Will there be room for both of us?" shot back the lovely.

James had many delusions about his irresistibility and over Pouilly Fuissé and Mobray Pie at a polo game – "the three great loves of my life!" – he came on rather clumsily to a beautiful rider.

"Where have you been all my life?" he asked.

"Well, for most of it, I wasn't even born," was the reply.

Lines have to be good and an experienced social fisherman knows that to reel in his catch he will have to be determined, but patient.

A strike is one thing. Landing the prize is another.

But to help you at least offer the proper bait, I'd like to recommend the following openers to you. They have all worked well for yours truly.

10. "I've dropped my Nobel Prize on the floor. I wonder if you'd mind helping me look for it?" This is a particularly good line with a youngish set in a crowded pub or bar. Unless you look like Einstein, the idea is outrageous. You obviously have a fair sense of humor. Make a woman laugh and she is a quarter of the way to being in love with you.

9. "Excuse me, I'm new in town. Do you have a fan club or should I start one?" This plays on a woman's vanity. After such a compliment, it's hard for her to tell you to take a hike. You will almost certainly have opened the door for some fun repartee. You can follow this up by asking her if she has a photo with her that she might care to autograph.

8. "I'm an undercover agent and I'm being watched. Let's go back to your place." Deliver this with a poker face. Use your eyes to suggest who might be watching you. This works more times than you'd think.

ACTUALLY I'M A SECRET AGENT WORKING UNDERCOVER!

7. "I can't think where it was. Yes, that dreadful wedding two weeks ago! Didn't I see you there." This is an old chestnut that can still work as an opener. There is a chance that the woman has met you before and the mention of a wedding seems innocent enough. You may spend some time trying to "remember" exactly where else it might have been that your paths crossed. If she likes you, she'll ask about "that dreadful wedding."

6. Sit down next to a woman in a singles bar and say: "Whose friend do you think is going to show up first? Like to bet a glass of wine on it?" The lovely creature won't feel threatened because she believes you truly are waiting for a date. She will also appreciate your giving her an easy way out. After a while she can say she is tired of waiting and can move on graciously.

5. "As soon as I saw the sensitivity in your eyes, I felt compelled to mingle. I have a doctorate in mingling." This is a good line for several reasons. Everyone likes to think they have a sensitive soul and to suggest that theirs is very obvious must certainly cause them to drop their guard a tad. Mingling is a nonthreatening word. Everyone knows it's perfectly safe to mingle because other people are around. There's also a strong hint that you have an education, another big plus. You'll certainly have generated some attention. Follow up the rebound.

4. On the dance floor, make small talk and then slip in: "I'm pretty old fashioned and have stereotyped views. When I saw you I thought you looked so pretty that I didn't think you could possibly be so intelligent." Extreme confidence is needed to deliver this line. You may be told to take a hike, or worse. But if it's slipped sincerely into chat, you might be cruising for the rest of the night.

3. "Do you mind turning your head so I can see your profile a little better? I'm an artist and I've got to find one more subject for my next show." A friend who couldn't paint the side of a barn has had tremendous success with this one. He is very confident and strokes his chin as he turns the lady's head into the light from the north.

2. "Pardon me young lady, I'm a comedian and I'm looking for new material. Could you please tell me some of the lines guys use when they come on to you?" This immediately wins a woman because you think she attracts a great deal of attention. Women also like guys who will take a chance on life and try to make other people laugh.

1. Try winding your window down at traffic lights and yelling across: "If my day turns out half as well as you look, I've got it made." This is a winning line, because how can anyone feel threatened when their foot is resting on the gas pedal and their engine is running? You have to react quickly if you get a bite, ask her name and the company she works for. You can look the firm up in the telephone book.

HOW YOU KNOW IF YOU HAVE A BITE

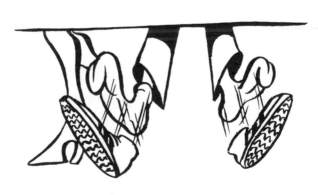

HOW YOU KNOW IF YOU HAVE A BITE

Eyes are the windows of the soul and you can always tell if a woman is interested by the eye contact you are making. No contact – nothing doing. Smiling eyes, lots of potential.

Here are 10 other signs that usually mean a woman is interested:

1. She stays in the vicinity while others mingle. (Make sure you are not standing on her dress.)

2. A compliment comes your way that keeps the conversation flowing, such as a remark about the tie you are wearing or how clean your baseball shirt is.

3. A constant reference to her single status.

4. Hints that she might be somewhere doing something by herself.

5. Relaxed body language, such as leaning towards you or touching your arm while making a point in a story.

6. She tells you stories about her past and mentions family.

SO, WHAT DO YOU THINK OF ME SO FAR ?

7. Laughs too much at your jokes that aren't that funny.

8. She gives you her card and tells you to call her about investment opportunities.

9. She asks about your favorite movie and tells you she like going to the theatre.

10. She grabs your crotch.

Here are a few tips that mean she's definitely not interested:

1. She writes your phone number on the sole of her shoe.

2. She walks away with a full glass saying she has to get another drink.

3. When you mention lunch, she says she goes home to feed her cat.

4. She tries to keep another person involved in conversation so you are never alone, and often breaks into a Mickey Mouse voice.

5. She tells you she is a lesbian and keeps looking over her shoulder to see if anyone more interesting is around.

6. She says she's from a foreign country that has an unusually high number of AIDS cases.

7. She gives you the weather office number when you request her telephone number.

8. She tells you she'll be right back and you spot her laughing with a Mel Gibson look-alike for an hour.

9. She puts her cigarette out in your drink.

10. She says the only time she'd sleep with you is when she's too lazy to take herself in hand.

LINES THAT ARE SO BAD . . . THEY MIGHT JUST WORK

1. My analyst told me to talk to three women a day; you look as if you'd be very easy to talk to.

2. Do you think we could have been soul mates in another life?

3. If someone told you you had a beautiful body, would you hold it against them?

4. What's your horoscope sign?

5. Would you like to see the back seat of my car?

6. There's a warm wind blowing the stars around and I really want to be with you tonight.

7. I'm terminally ill and only have 24 hours to live.

8. You look like a princess without a tiara.

9. What do you like for breakfast?

10. How about a game of couch rugby?

PARTY IDEAS

PARTY IDEAS

Throwing a good party puts you in a special club. Women know that a man who throws a good bash is creative, has organizational skills, is confident socially and has friends in many walks of life.

Anyone can say: "Hey, bring a case of beer over and we'll order some pizza." But it takes you to put that special spin on the evening.

Here are a few working suggestions that you can embellish. Once you have the germ of an idea, set your imagination free. Be a Party Poet.

An invite in the mail, well ahead of the event, is the best way to request people's presence. This is especially true if some preparation is involved, such as making a plateful of food or a toga.

While the following themes all involve alcohol, it's a good idea to have a tasty, eye-catching, nonalcoholic punch or other beverage available.

How do you end a party when you have had enough? Telling everyone the coffee is on is one way to do it. But handing bores their coats often brings better results.

Remember also that as a host, you have the responsibility of making sure people get home safely. You may have to drive them. Or offer them your bed.

YUCCA FLATS

This party concept dates back to the Spanish-American War, when Colonel "Wild Bill" Culpepper threw a zinger of a party in his fort just south of Santa Fe. He knew a Mexican attack was imminent, but he wasn't going to let that interfere with his lifestyle.

He invited everyone to throw what white grog they had left into a barrel already laden with local fruit, such as oranges, lemons and grapefruit. And then he had the lovely Rosa Garcia, the toast of the cantina over the hill, trample the concoction down with her pretty bare feet.

The libation that came from the barrel was so good that the Mexicans sought to join in the ensuing revelry. A truce broke out that lasted for years.

Culpepper's men poured mainly local tequila into the barrel, but any type of white liquor is good. White rum, gin, vodka and white wine can all be used. The idea is to get people to bring their favorite potion and the amount they think they will consume.

85

It is poured into a giant clean plastic garbage can (large coolers also work well) loaded with oranges, limes, lemons, pineapple, watermelon or cantaloupe, whatever you care for or can pick up at a good price. Cut the fruit into fairly small squares.

Chuck in some ice, like a bag full.

Next, you must invite a woman with a good sense of humor and absolutely divine legs to step into the barrel and stamp the mix together, much the way they used to make wine. Wash her feet publicly. Turn it into a ceremony and have fun.

It's probably a good idea to tip a favorite girl-friend off that she is going to be invited to do this. Your cocktails just won't taste the same if you have to do it yourself.

If your concoction is too strong – the crowd will probably yell that it isn't – you can add some mix that you just happen to have on hand.

Plastic glasses are a must. And have several ladles on hand. You will be amazed, as Colonel Culpepper was, at just how many "experts" there are in your group who know exactly what this one-of-a-kind brew should taste like.

The fruit will suck up all kinds of alcohol and some say it makes a great fruit cocktail the fol-lowing day. You will often find that a few friends have enjoyed your hospitality overnight and will want to pour a few more bottles in and keep going.

The secret is to make sure the plastic garbage can is sterilized, or darn close to it. Swirling out with boiling water is one way of kissing all the bad bacteria good night.

Have a couple of plastic, 60-ounce jugs on hand to make pouring your brew easy. You will usual-ly find you have a major social phenomena on your hands long before the party "proper" begins.

KEG PARTY

Never underestimate the power of a keg party.

Young men reaching for the first rung on the corporate ladder know that producing an endless river of pints, inexpensively, for peers can do them nothing but good.

Truckers, used to the thirsty work of making sure their loads get down the highway no matter what the weather, often get religious when handed a foaming pint from a newly tapped keg.

And retired executives, scurrying home late from the golf course, wipe back a tear at the mention of a keg party as they recall the fire in their undergraduate loins.

A keg party isn't as hard to throw as it was in the old days, because you no longer have to smash that old rod in with a hammer and blacken your thumb before partying commences.

Technology has given us the easy-to-use pump. But a word of warning. Some seem to think that the more elbow grease you put into the pump, the faster beer is going to flow. That's not true. Pumping quickly only produces more foam. Pump at a pace you could hold for the rest of your life.

People are often reluctant to loan or rent pumps. Spending $50 on buying one might be a sound investment.

Most breweries and hotels will sell you a keg. A 2,000-ounce keg is the standard size and should supply enough beer for between 30 to 35 people. That's unless your guests are the local constabulary or a women's rugby club.

It's mandatory to let your keg sit for at least 30 minutes before opening or you will be washed down the street in a river of foam. An hour or two is better.

You are going to have to find a way to keep the keg cool, of course. Taking all but the bottom shelf out of a big refrigerator and popping it in there is one way of doing it.

Another good method is to stand it in one of those old galvanized tubs that is full of ice.

If neither of those methods works for you, try standing it in a triple layer of garbage bags and then stuffing ice right to the bottom of the bags. Tie the garbage bags around the keg with a string.

Some thought is needed as to where you are going to stand the keg. It goes without saying that you aren't going to put it on a new carpet. You may never get your damage deposit back.

Garages, patios and uncarpeted basements are made for keg parties. Remember to use plastic glasses.

If you are lucky enough to enjoy a keg party in the ambiance of your basement, you can probably hose down the floor later and get rid of that wonderful smell of stale beer.

Nothing is finer with draught beer than a barbecue. If you are paying for it, consider everyone's

88   favorite, tube steaks (hot dogs!).

You should launch the evening with lots of nibblies, such as pretzels, chips and peanuts. If you are throwing an affair in your garage or some other spot where the floor can easily be swept, consider a 5-pound bag of peanuts. There's nothing quite so decadent and enjoyable as dropping peanut shells on the floor. Do it in your house or apartment and you will be scooping up peanut shell fragments for at least a year.

JIMMY BUFFET PARTY

We've all been to Margaritaville several times and are permanently nostalgic about sipping a cocktail under the palms as the sun goes down.

A Jimmy Buffet party can signal the beginning of the end of summer, when the women can dress scantily and show off their tans. Or it can be thrown in the depths of winter when our souls need a boost of spiritual sunshine.

If you can party outdoors, use patio furniture and tables with umbrellas. Try and come up with some palm trees, make them if you have to.

If you are throwing the party indoors, clear out as much furniture as you decently can, because when you set the mood with old time rock 'n' roll and Jimmy Buffet, you know people are going to dance.

It's time for margaritas, piña colada, rum, fruit punches and all those cocktails that call for fruity drinks.

It's a time for the type of outfit you'd wear to a "Tacky Tourist" party, the gaudier the better.

And it's time for a limbo contest.

If you can get your hands on one of those guns they use in bars for pop, fill it with margaritas, pressure up with some CO_2 and wander around filling up glasses from your hand-held nozzle.

Not that we are saying to try it, in case anyone drowns, but an old favorite at a Jimmy Buffet party is the Upside Down Margarita. It's best if you have an old barber's chair handy, but assuming you don't, get someone to lean back over a stout chair.

Next, have the person close his eyes and open his mouth and tell him not to swallow until you tell him to.

Fill his mouth up to about half-tongue level with tequila and round out the full-tongue mark with Triple Sec. Top up with lime mix until the mouth is full.

Tell him that when he opens his eyes, he is to swirl the mixture around and then swallow.

For some reason, this ritual seems to work better if he opens his eyes and sees a good looking lady profiled above him, smoking bottles in either hand.

That's the traditional Upside Down Margarita. There are varieties, such as going with straight tequila.

It's worth finding a novelty shop that sells those little umbrellas you can put in cocktails. Your local manager can probably point you in the right direction. Drinks always look better if they have an orange slice and cherry floating in them. It reflects well on your creativity and world experience.

TOGA PARTY

This well-tried favorite is easy to prepare for and can be relatively inexpensive while looking lavish.

Begin by telling everyone they have to wear togas. The guys can make them out of sheets and the women look great in pillowcases.

Push formal furniture into one room and lock the door. Throw mattresses and pillows everywhere. There's going to be a lot of rolling on the floor. But also designate a dancing area where nothing is likely to be knocked over.

Garlands can be made from materials found in your parents' boxes of Christmas decorations. There are always far too many of those green garland-type things knocking around anyway. Use the green twist ties from grocery supermarkets to hold pieces in place.

Supply lots of grapes and other types of fruits, as well as some cheeses and loaves of bread. They all go down well with red wine.

Don't spend a fortune on vintage wine. Find a good, inexpensive Cabernet Sauvignon with lots of body and fruit, buy it in bulk and pour it into jugs. The Chileans, Portuguese and South Africans have lots of gutsy, dry, inexpensive cabernets on the market.

Batches of Spicy Caesars also tie in well to the evening and can be made in advance and kept in the refrigerator.

A good nonalcoholic punch is a must, as always.

Well into the evening, and to keep up the fun, try serving chocolate-dipped strawberries with white sparking wine.

Think of ways to enhance the evening by using props. See if you can rent Ben Hur from the video store and have it playing on your TV. Search the local pawn shops or garden supply companies to see if you can get your hands on statues of naked people, especially Greek models with their arms broken off. Use the office copier to blow up some pictures from encyclopedias of chariot races and centurions.

HOT TUB PARTY

Check the Yellow Pages, a hot tub rental company can make you the toast of your friends any weekend, winter or summer.

People know they are going to have fun in a hot tub and they don't expect to enjoy fine dining with exotic wines.

Keep things simple. A steak or chicken barbecue works well with a hot tub party. You can bake potatoes in advance and prepare a gigantic Caesar salad.

Baked beans usually go well with this type of food, but be warned that the bubbles floating to the surface of the hot tub might not all be from the water jets.

There is one serious warning that must accompany any suggestion of a hot tub party: no one must ever be left alone in the hot tub. And keep an eye on the amount your friends have had to drink. Too much partying can be a recipe for disaster in hot, relaxing water. People have died.

It also goes without saying that you should never allow bottles or glass in the hot tub area. Use metal or plastic only.

If you live in northern climes and enjoy snow in the water, encourage your guests to take a roll in the snow before plunging back into the tub. This is invigorating and maintains most people with some semblance of sobriety.

Leave lots of towels around and suggest to your friends that they might want to bring a bathrobe.

Assign changing rooms for the sexes, unless you know all your friends very well. Make sure the women's changing room is as near to the tub as possible. Serious partiers report that after a dip, women spend a lot of time with pencils and powder.

As the host, it is perfectly in order for you to take a snorkel and mask into the tub and check out what is happening beneath the waves. It's amazing where 10 people's hands can explore.

THE ULTIMATE NEW YEAR'S EVE PARTY

A good New Year's party will be talked about for years. And planning is everything. There are usually a million things happening at New Year's, so it's important to send out a classy invite well ahead of time. People can then plan to celebrate with you.

New Year's is the one time you can be as formal as you want. There's no doubt you are probably seeking to impress someone special, perhaps even propose. If the evening has those implications, consider making it a black tie affair.

If it's a friend who plans to do the proposing, his sweetheart will want to thank you forever. "Charles proposed to me at Jim's black tie affair on New Year's," she'll say for the rest of her life.

Lots of hors-d'oeuvres are a must. If you have the time, make them yourself. If you have the money, have them made. If you have good friends, ask them to bring a plateful each.

Serve hot and cold tasty treats. Items you can put on toothpicks and served by the trayful will be snapped up.

The party goers should be able to watch the old year slipping away on the hands of a well-placed clock. A good host will have lots of balloons around, with streamers and noise makers for all.

Think out the type of music you would enjoy dancing to well ahead of time. Make sure your designated dance area is free from obstruction and that nothing is likely to get broken.

Offer a good variety of libations early in the evening, but when midnight arrives, Dom Perignon champagne should be served.

Now, I'm not suggesting you break into your life savings. The best thing to do here is to have your well-heeled friends give you the bottles of Dom Perignon they have emptied at weddings, christenings and other special occasions. Or you may have a friend, who is a well-placed waiter or bartender at a local fine-dining restaurant, who can get his hands on a few empties.

Having poured some sparkling wine into Dom Perignon bottles, you organize some "popping" sounds in the kitchen and then come rushing out with bottles of Dom and a tray or two full of glasses. Tests have shown that at this time of night, no one will be wise to the fact they are drinking a very good Spanish imitation of one of France's greatest champagnes.

If there was ever a night for a host to stay sober and on top of things, this is it. On your invitation, it might be worth mentioning that you plan to take guests' car keys at the door and return them after a fun test for sobriety. A tragic accident is no way for anyone to start the New Year.

If someone looks a tad worse for wear, as a good friend you must drive them home or offer them a bed, which might be yours.

Your only alternative is to invite Charles, the nephew of your great aunt Gertrude's second cousin twice removed. He may be a pain, but as the owner of a van he loves **97** showing off. Get him to make a milk run and drop off those who might pose a threat to the public and themselves.

Robert Burns' Auld Lang Syne (old long ago) is traditionally sung just after midnight, or certainly before the party breaks up. It's sad but true that not many people know the correct words to what is considered by many to be the national anthem of the human race.

Here then is the chorus and first and last verse of this great Scottish song. You may want to copy and pass them around, but people always think they know the words or are so used to faking them that it doesn't matter. They murder the song anyway. At least, as the perfect host, you can keep them on track.

Chorus
And for auld lang syne, my jo,
 For auld lang syne,
We'll tak a cup o' kindness yet,
 For auld land syne.

Should auld acquaintance be forgot,
 And never brought to mind?
Should auld acquaintance be forget,
 And the days o' lang syne?

And there's a hand, my trusty fierce! (chum)
 And gie's (give me) a hand o' thine!
And we'll take a right gude-willy waught, (good will drink)
 For auld lang syne.

PACK YOUR BAGS PARTY

This is an easy-to-arrange party with a lot of inherent energy. Price out a trip to somewhere popular, such as Mexico. Work out the number of people coming to the party and divide that into the cost.

For example, if 150 people are expected and each chips in $10 a head, that would give you $1,500 to play with.

Do this off season and you can get some wonderful deals.

The chosen holiday destination, say Mexico, Hawaii or the Caribbean, becomes the theme of the party.

Everyone brings a suitcase with some survival gear and after the draw to find the winner, they are driven to the airport for an immediate departure.

It's wild to be partying with a group that knows two people are headed to an exotic destination before the evening is over. It's amazing the number of people you'll find who want to get into the action for $10 a head.

And what better way to get to know someone you have been dying to know a little better than by sitting next to her on an aircraft.

It doesn't have to be an overseas destination to make this party work. At stake might be a trip to a football or baseball playoff game. Or it might be a goose-hunting, fishing, golf or gambling trip that's on the line. The world is yours.

ULTIMATE SURPRISE PARTY

There can be few people who don't become a little suspicious when their birthday comes around.
"Will they try to pull a fast one on me?" The
only thing worse than being surprised is that no
one gives a darn.

As a man-about-town, you must often be the one
to make the arrangements to surprise a wonderful deserving woman.

A surprise party doesn't have to be limited to
birthdays. Graduations, promotions, anniver-
saries, a success, or moving, apartments or
home, are just some of the other events that may
be worthy of a sneak-attack party.

The secret of planning such an event is to think
well ahead. We're talking months, if possible.
The "victim" is then far less likely to catch on.

If this is for a woman in your life, get someone
she knows and trusts, like your mother, her
mother, an aunt, a close personal friend
100 or her boss, to invite her to supper,

bowling, to visit family or some other enterprise that will effectively commit her and put her off guard. You know what will work.

Next, you must decide where the party is to be held and what form it will take. If you're stuck for a venue for a party you'd perhaps like to throw for a girlfriend at work, consider renting a small hall. There are lots of community-type halls about that can comfortably accommodate between 100 and 150 people. Divide the costs between your colleagues.

If the party is for your partner, it's probably best to have it your place. But other venues might be a favorite restaurant or pub or a friend's place. If the woman is an avid tennis player, bowler, blues fan, opera buff or skier, other ideas might suggest themselves.

If there are a few conspirators or guests at the party, several can be primed to deliver a good "roast" story. Tell them to make the stories as embarrassing as possible.

Naked photos of the subject as an infant always go over well. Perhaps have them blown up to poster size.

A nice, thoughtful present is also a must. Don't make it lingerie guys, especially if her close friends and parents are there. That's for later when she can truly show you how much she cares.

Another tip: Don't cover a birthday cake with lots of candles. The icing will melt. Try one sparkler for each decade.

PARTY CHECKLIST

ICE CONTAINERS

CORKSCREW

INVITATION CARDS

PLASTIC GLASSES

MOUTH WASH & GUM

COFFEE

CAN OR BOTTLE OPENER

MUSIC TAPES & C.D's.

SODA & TONIC WATERS

ROLAIDS

SHOOTER GLASSES

STRAWS

A STRAINER

TOILET PAPER

NON-ALCOHOLIC DRINKS

LIST

STRAWS

ASH TRAYS

COOL-CAT MUSIC

CAR KEYS

PARTY CHECKLIST

Nothing impresses the fair sex more than a man in control of destiny. And a party is the perfect time to show the lady in your life, or perhaps about to come into your life, that you have great foresight and conceptual skills.

You will lose major points if she pokes her head around the washroom door and yells: "You're out of toilet paper."

But toilet paper is a little further down your checklist. The first thing to do is sort out a date and them make a list of who is coming to your soirée. Pop suitable invitations in the mail. That's class.

A tip about supplies comes from General Montgomery Culpepper, who was involved in the logistical planning of the world's greatest movable meal, D-Day.

"When I go skiing in the mountains," he once said, "I always check my equipment from my feet up, mentally ticking off each item that I will need."

"So too, I handle an invasion force or cocktail party. I mentally run through the scenario and take care of any inadequacy that presents itself."

When people walk through your door, you need a place to put their coats. If it's a fairly good-sized gathering, you are not going to be able to hang everyone's coat in the closet. A bedroom should be designated, where coats, scarves and bags can be left. (It might be worth checking from time to time that no one is sleeping on top of them.)

The next think you will want to do is offer your guests a drink. If it's a smallish party, you probably have enough glasses to suffice. If it's a bigger bash, consider renting glasses from a party supply company. They don't charge a great deal, but you do have to pay for breakage.

Don't forget if it's an active crowd you are entertaining, that plastic glasses might serve better.
This is especially true if
people might take their
shoes off, such as at
a pool or hot tub
party. If you go with
plastic, hide your
glasses in the base-
ment. There's no
point in finding
your favorite
antique crystal
Scotch glass broken.

If you are buying a keg at a brewery, ask if they
throw in plastic glasses free of charge. Some do.

Beer bottles also pose a threat and are out. Go
with aluminum cans. A bonus is they chill faster.
Keep on the right side of your environmentally-
conscious friends by having a garbage can clear-
ly marked: "Cans and bottles."

Support your favorite charity with the proceeds
from empties, or buy a bottle of vodka for a
Bloody Mary to help fight the hangover.

You know what you plan to serve in terms of
alcohol, but don't forget a good supply of such
things as: celery salt, salt, pepper, Tabasco,
Worcestershire sauce and a bottle of Chinese hot
sauce for those who say they can never get a
drink hot enough. Have a few drinking straws on
hand.

A good supply of mix shouldn't be overlooked.
You'll probably need orange, Clamato and
grapefruit juice (buy large tin cans); ginger ale;
Coke or Pepsi; Sprite, 7-Up or some other type
of uncola. A bottle of soda and tonic may be
called for.

There should be some diet mix for those who
want to show off and pretend their drinks aren't
laden with calories.

Make sure the bar is not in the same area as food
or there will be total congestion and drinks will
be spilled on the floor regularly.

A big supply of paper towels is a necessity, to heck with serviettes.

Think carefully about where you are going to put the beer supply. An empty refrigerator of course is perfect. But the chances are, yours is being used for any number of other important things.

Next thought is a bath tub. Beer can be dumped in the tub with a few bags of ice poured over it. But rule this suggestion out if the bath tub is in the only washroom in the house. Women tend to get into the facilities during a party and tie it up for a while. A guy could die of thirst before he gets another cool one.

A big garbage can on the patio also works well. Again, just dump some ice on your suds.

A good punch or some other nonalcoholic drinks must also receive careful consideration.

Plan to run down your food stock in the refrigerator. It's amazing the number of people who will feel at home in your kitchen and eat anything they find.

Men aren't known to be good bathroom cleaners, but give this chore your best shot. Promise yourself a reward for doing a really good job.

Never put that blue stuff in the toilet tank. A guy not feeling well and talking into the telephone will find his shirt stained from the splatter.

Some great music is a must, but try not to use your favorite tapes or CDs. They can be easily damaged. Suggest people bring some music. Or try finding what you want at the local library.

Don't forget the toilet paper. Lock up your valuables and provide a major supply of ashtrays, to save your furniture and rugs.

Don't put food out at the beginning of the evening, other than a few nibblies such as potato or tortilla chips. Major delicacies will disappear immediately. Present them at about 10 or 11 p.m.

There should be a good supply of coffee on hand. This option becomes a must later in the evening.

Other things you will probably need:

- A shooter glass for measuring
- A bottle opener, a can opener and a corkscrew
- Ice containers
- A knife for cutting lemons and taking the top off wine bottles
- A strainer
- Towels and sponges
- Coasters
- Mosquito repellent if the affair is to grace your yard in the summer
- A supply of mouth wash and chewing gum

As host, you must stay reasonably straight and make sound decisions about whether someone should be invited to stay for another cup of coffee, be sent home in a cab or enjoy a bed for the night at your place.

It's not a bad ideas to get everyone's car keys when they arrive. This might be difficult as people today see this much as a gunfighter viewed having to check in his Colt in the Wild West. Be creative about it. Tell people their car keys make them eligible for a draw. Do a caricature of them as they leave.

The last thing you need on your mind for the rest of your life is the thought that a friend died on the way home from your party.

Parties are a wonderful way of keeping in touch with friends, meeting new ones and getting rid of the stress built up by the daily hustle and bustle of life. But as General Culpepper said: "Throwing a party without thinking is like shooting without taking aim."

GLASSES

BACHELOR'S GLASSES

JAM JAR

STYROFOAM CUP

CHIPPED MUG

PITCHER

PLASTIC CUP

TOASTS

TOASTS

Women love a polished, spiritually well-rounded man, who can come up with a toast that adds to the occasion.

If you are naturally glib, or a lawyer, read no further. I don't intent to waste my time on you. But if you need a couple of easy-to-remember toasts for those preg-nant moments, here are a few that may come in handy.

Short, Sweet and Intimate

I have known many,
Liked a few
Loved one -
Here's to you.

Here's to love, the only fire against which there is no insurance. (This should be spoken while maintaining strong eye contact.)

May your voyage through life be as
     happy and free
as the dancing waves on the deep
     blue sea.

At the start of an evening on the town!
Here's head first, in a foaming glass!
Here's head first, to a lively lass!
(English toast)

For the Woman Who Likes Dry Humor
May all your labors be in vein.
(An old Yorkshire Miners' Toast)

For the Woman Who Likes Wet Humor
How beautiful the water is!
To me 'tis wondrous sweet -
For bathing purposes and such;
But liquor's better neat.

For The Romantic
Were't the last drop in the
   well,
As I gasp'd upon the
   brink,
Ere my fainting spirit
   fell,
'Tis to thee that I would
   drink.

Here's to Love; a thing
   divine,
Description makes it but
   the less.
'Tis what we feel, but
   cannot define
'Tis what we know but cannot express.

In case a Glass of Sincerity is Called For
Here's to your good health,
and your family's good health,
and may you all live long and prosper.

Here's to the one and only one,
   And may that one be she,
Who loves but one and only one,
   And may that one be me.

**This next one works well on foreign ladies
who don't know you cribbed it from a well-
known poem.**

Drink to me only with thine eyes,
   And I will pledge with mine;
Or leave a kiss but in the cup,
   And I'll not look for wine.

At Her Place
If I drink too much of your liquor,
   And should be foolish enough to get tight,
Would you be a perfect lady,
   And see that I get home all right?

For Those Who Wish to Lose Bachelorhood
Here's to the wings of love -
May they never molt a feather,
till my big boots and your little shoes,
Are under the bed together.

Health to the bold and dashing coquette,
    Who careth not for me;
Whose heart, untouched by
love as yet,
    Is wild and fancy free.

Before a Night on the Town
There was an old hen
And she had a wooden leg,
And every damned morning
She laid another egg;
She was the best damned
  chicken
On the whole darn farm -
And another little drink
Wouldn't do us any harm.
(American folk song.)

Drink! for you know not
  whence
you came, nor why:
Drink! for you know not why you go nor where.
(From Omar Khayyam's *Rubaiyat.*)

Drink today, and drown all sorrow,
You shall perhaps not do it tomorrow.

When You Suspect She's Met Another
Here's a toast that I want to give
    To a fellow I'll never know;
To the fellow who's going to take my place
When it's time for me to go.

This is a great one when you have been asked to do some chore on a particularly hot or cold day and want to make a point.

Ho! stand to your glasses steady!
    'tis all we have left to prize.
A cup to the dead already,
    Hurrah for the next man that dies.

This is a good one if you've been accused of chauvinism:

Here's to the woman whose heart
    and whose soul
Are the light and life of each spell
    we pursue;
Whether sunn'd at the tropics or
    chilled at the pole,
If woman be there, there is happiness too.

THE CAT IS HIC TOASTED

HANGOVER
CURES

HANGOVER CURES

It was 3,000 years ago that Confucius Culpepper distilled rice and millet in China and produced sautchoo, the world's first alcoholic drink.

And the search for a cure has been going on ever since.

The only person who knew the perfect alcohol antidote was Jeeves, the valet who looked after upper-crust Bertie Wooster.

He answered an employment advertisement, found Wooster totally hungover, mixed a special concoction that instantly cured his potential employer and won himself a job.

But Jeeves and Wooster are the figments of P.G. Wodehouse's imagination, and the author would never say for sure what it was that Jeeves mixed.

So we are left with suggestions such as those from Turkish cook, Remzi tok, who recommends iskembe (tripe) soup. And columnist Nicole Parton: "Try covering both feet with cucumber slices."

Many a Polar Bear Club's New Year's swim began as a search for a hangover. But that seems a bit drastic and there are other avenues to

explore.

Here are a few:

Boston hotelier Jose Campo: "A slightly different hair of the dog – heat orange juice with some lemon, honey and a little cognac."

Hawaiian voodoo tradition: "Stick 13 pins into the cork of the bottle you were drinking from."

Chic Simple Components Bath Book: "Put five to 10 drops of oil of cloves into your bath water. While in the bath, quarter a lemon and rub the juicy side under each armpit. Follow by eating 10 strawberries, if you have a headache, or drinking a cup of ginger tea if you have an upset stomach."

Jazz musician Eddie Condon: "Take the juice of two quarts of whisky!"

Diarist Samuel Pepys: "One quart of orange juice laced with sugar."

Dean Martin: "Stay drunk."

Toronto Deejay Ron Christie: "Look at a photo of Tammy Bakker. You will be shocked sober. It only takes a minute."

English Middle Ages tip: "Take one spiced eel sprinkled with almonds."

Vancouver Island fisherman's suggestion: "Oysters, honey and ginger with a can of Kokanee beer."

Dr. Harold Kant, University of Toronto pharmacologist: "The best thing is to sleep it off. If you can't, take headache medication, eat lightly and get some fresh air."

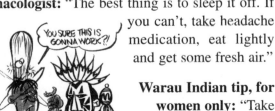

Warau Indian tip, for women only: "Take your mate when you come upon him the worse for wear and tie him mummy-like in a hammock until the siege is over."

New Hampshire hotelier Fritz Koeppel: "This never fails. Take the eyes of three Alpine owls and mix with tomato juice, a raw egg and Remy Martin. By the time you have finished arguing with the SPCA about importing owl's eyes, you'll find your hangover has gone.

Sam Abouhassan, tailor to the likes of Wayne Gretzky and Glen Sather of the National Hockey League: "A couple of shots of ouzo fixes me up..."

Dr. O'Donahue Culpepper: "Attack each symptom separately – Aspirin for headache, herbal tea for queasy stomach and naps for exhaustion. You should be ready to go again by sundown."

Christain Graefe, Finnish consul in Alberta, Canada: "Pour a bottle of Finlandia vodka onto the sauna coals in a cabin where a dozen people are using space designed for three or four. Inhale deeply. This is a custom dating back to the 1939 Finnish Winter War, which saw soldiers sent to the front without proper supplies. Men crammed into saunas to sniff vodka to make it go as far as possible. This is absolutely true."

W.C. Fields: "Always carry a flagon of whisky in case of 'snakebite.' Furthermore, also carry a small snake."

The truth is probably somewhere between all of the above. Everyone has a different alcohol tolerance level. So if the cure to a hangover is prevention, it's up to everyone to know their comfortable limit.

There's no doubt that eating before drinking slows down alcohol absorption and that drinking water, juice or mix during a session also helps.

A glass of water and an Aspirin before you go to bed can work wonders.

Next day, try a cup of hot water with a tablespoon of honey, or honey by itself. Progress to other liquids, such as fruit juice. Coca-Cola is great, especially with ice cream.

Bicarbonate of soda or Alka-Seltzer might help settle a scandalized stomach and stifle a headache.

The jury is out on whether "the hair of the dog" really helps. After all, your body can only handle so much alcohol.

If your stomach will stand it, there's no doubt a big meal with lots of meat, salt, carbohydrates, sauces, pickles and vegetables will replenish stores the body needs.

As a bachelor, you will probably identify with author F. Scott Fitzgerald, who once wrote: "The hangover becomes a part of the day as well-allowed for as the Spanish siesta."

INDEX

121

THE BACHELOR'S GUIDE™ TEAM

YARDLEY JONES, ILLUSTRATOR

Yardley Jones is an award-winning, internationally syndicated cartoonist, whose work hangs in the homes and offices of Premiers, Prime Ministers, U.S. Presidents and members of the Royal Family.

He has worked with newspapers across Canada and the National Archives has acquired for posterity all of his earlier cartoons still in his possession.

His work has been featured in several books, including *The Bachelor's Guide™ To Ward Off Starvation*, and he has also shown millions of people how to draw through his North American television series, *Cartooning with Yardley Jones*.

But while Jones still enjoys poking fun with his pen, he is now very active in his first love, watercolors and his work has been featured in many shows.

NICK LEES, WRITER

Glasgow born, Nick Lees is a journalist and author who has sipped tequila at sea with Mexican shrimp boat fishermen; compared vodkas with Russian soldiers in St. Petersburg and searched for a hangover cure in Crete after imbibing what had seemed like a rather fine Greek red wine the previous evening. While he believes he found the perfect Chinese riesling to complement the dog he had in Beijing and a full dry sake that went well with sea cucumber in Japan, Lees always returns to a single malt Scotch after dinner.

He is presently employed by the *Edmonton Journal*, a classy Canadian daily that has sought ingenious ways to get rid of him. He has taken part in an ascent on Canada's highest peak, Mt. Logan; parachuted with the Canadian Airborne Regiment; driven in demolition derbies and run marathons in the Arctic and in Greece with Yardley Jones, his adopted stepfather.

CLARENCE SHIELDS, COORDINATOR

Clarence Shields was born to be in the restaurant and bar business. Upon completing university, he joined his father as a grill cook (hamburger flipper) at the family A & W in the wilds of boom town northern Alberta. It was the first A & W in Canada to exceed one million dollars in sales, an accomplishment he and his father repeated for the following three years.

Over the last 20 years, Clarence has coordinated the planning, construction and operation of more than a dozen restaurants, bars and hotels throughout Alberta, Canada, and the islands of the Caribbean (a whole other story).

Clarence loves people and has a talent for turning concepts and dreams into reality. A fondness for good food and libations prompted him to spearhead the development of a series of books designed with a truly male perspective. Clarence loves making it happen. His enthusiasm for life is contagious and a motivation to others.

The Bachelor's Guide™ Survival Cooking For Kids

by Clarence "Culinary" Culpepper

Recipes that kids enjoy (and dads can cook) are combined with creative activity suggestions and practical survival tips for shopping and travelling with kids. Satisfying, easy-to-make, kid-oriented snacks plus breakfast, lunch and supper recipes; games to play with the whole family; inexpensive, entertaining activities that dads can do with the kids and, of course, the sparkling humor of Yardley Jones' cartoons.

Retail $16.95   7" x 10"
160 pages   cartoons throughout
                  wire coil bound

The Bachelor's Guide™ To Ward Off Starvation

by Clarence "Culinary" Culpepper

The ultimate bachelor's cookbook, written by bachelors for bachelors. This book is educational, entertaining and enables the budding chef to feed himself and to impress the women in his life (and his buddies). Recipes were developed by a professional chef for easy preparation. Brilliant cartoons by Yardley Jones, one of Canada's foremost illustrators and cartoonists, add wit and spice throughout. An ideal cookbook for men. A great gift.

Retail $18.95   7" x 10"
176 pages   100 cartoons throughout
                  wire coil bound

124

Share
The Bachelor's Guide™ To Libations
with a friend

Order *The Bachelor's Guide™ To Libations* at $12.95 per book plus $4.00 (total order) for shipping and handling.

Bachelor's Guide™
  To Libations _____ x $12.95 = $ ____

Bachelor's Guide™
  To Ward Off Starvation ____ x $18.95 = $ ____

Bachelor's Guide™, Survival
  Cooking for Kids _____ x $16.95 = $ ____

Postage and handling _____ = $ _4.00_

Subtotal _____ = $ ____

In Canada add 7% GST __(Subtotal x .07) = $ ____

Total enclosed _____ = $ ____

U.S. prices:
The Bachelor's Guide™ To Libations $9.95
The Bachelor's Guide™ $14.95
Bachelor's Guide™, Cooking for Kids $12.95

Price is subject to change.

NAME:_____

STREET: _____

CITY: _____

PROV./STATE _____

COUNTRY: _____

POSTAL CODE/ZIP _____

Please make cheque or money order payable to:
Normac Publishing Ltd.
4104 - 149 Street
Edmonton, Alberta
Canada   T6H 5L9

For fund raising or volume rates,
contact **Normac Publishing Ltd.**
1-800-691-3056   Canada/U.S.A.

Please allow 3-4 weeks for delivery

125

GIFT IDEAS MEN

Great GIFTS IDEAS for MEN!

CANADIAN NATIONAL BEST SELLERS!

☆ THE BACHELOR'S GUIDE™ "TO WARD OFF STARVATION"

☆ THE BACHELOR'S GUIDE™ "TO LIBATIONS BAR GUIDE"

☆ THE BACHELOR'S GUIDE™ "SURVIVAL COOKING FOR KIDS"

☆ THE BACHELOR'S GUIDE™ COOKING KIT

☆ THE BACHELOR'S GUIDE™ LIBATIONS BAR KIT

☆ THE BACHELOR'S GUIDE™ GOLF KIT

ALL YEAR 'ROUND!